I1029700

PHYSICIAN RECRUITMENT
Strategies
That
Work

Suzanne M. Lewitt
President
Medical Career Services
Encino, California

AN ASPEN PUBLICATION®
Aspen Publishers, Inc.
Rockville, Maryland
London
1982

Library of Congress Cataloging in Publication Data

Lewitt, Suzanne McNeely.
Physician recruitment.

Includes index.
1. Physicians—Recruiting. 2. Hospitals—Medical
staff—Recruiting. 3. Physicians—United States—
Recruiting. I. Title.
RA972.L45   362.1'1'0683   82-4088
ISBN: 0-89443-693-7   AACR2

Publisher: John Marozsan
Editorial Director: Michael Brown
Managing Editor: Margot Raphael
Editorial Services: Scott Ballotin
Printing and Manufacturing: Debbie Swarr

Library of Congress Catalog Card Number: 82-4088
ISBN: 0-89443-693-7

Printed in the United States of America

2 3 4 5

Table of Contents

Preface vii

Acknowledgments ix

PART I—   DEVELOPMENT OF THE PHYSICIAN
            RECRUITMENT PROCESS 1

Chapter 1— **Marketing Strategy and the Planning Committee** 3
            The Marketing Process 3
            Establishing the Planning Committee 4

Chapter 2— **Determining the Need for Physicians** 7
            Quantitative Analysis 8
            Qualitative Analysis 17

Chapter 3— **Market Analysis** 21
            Environment 21
            Marketing Problems 24
            Opportunities 26
            Summary 27

Chapter 4— **Recruitment Program Options** 33
            Selection Criteria 33
            Program Options 37
            Summary 45

Chapter 5— **Recruitment Firms**...**47**
Types of Recruitment Firms 47
Assessment Criteria 49
The Working Relationship between the Firm and the
Hospital...53

Chapter 6— **Financial Aspects**...**57**
Financial Assistance...58
Nonhospital-Based Physician Contractual
Arrangements 67
Hospital-Based Physician Agreements 74
Appendix 6-A 76

PART II— **IMPLEMENTATION OF THE PHYSICIAN
RECRUITMENT PROCESS—EXTERNAL
RECRUITMENT** **103**

Chapter 7— **The External Recruitment Committee**..................**105**
Responsibilities...105
Member Role Descriptions.................................106
Summary 110

Chapter 8— **Physician Sources**...**111**
Residency Programs and Medical Schools....................111
Professional Journals 112
Medical Meetings and Licensing Boards 113
Other Physicians 113
Foreign Medical Graduates.................................114
Appendix 8-A 116
Appendix 8-B 121
Appendix 8-C 123
Appendix 8-D 126
Appendix 8-E 131
Appendix 8-F 135

Chapter 9— **Location Preferences**...**145**
Key Factors 145
Summary 148

Chapter 10— **The Preinterview Process**...**151**

    Basic Steps 151
    Summary 156
    Appendix 10-A.. 157

Chapter 11— **The Interview Process** **161**

    Basic Elements 161
    Summary 167

Chapter 12— **Follow-Up Steps and Strategies** **169**

    Follow-Up Tasks 169
    The Transition Period...................................... 171
    Retention of the Physician 173

PART III— **IMPLEMENTATION OF THE PHYSICIAN RECRUITMENT PROCESS—INTERNAL RECRUITMENT** **177**

Chapter 13— **The Internal Recruitment Committee**...............**179**

    Administrator 180
    Medical Staff Members..................................... 181
    Community Members 182
    Governing Board Member................................. 182

Chapter 14— **Retention of the Active Staff**............................**185**

    The Active Medical Staff Profile....................... 185
    Interviews with Active Medical Staff Members 188
    Summary 190

Chapter 15— **Nonactive Staff Utilization** **191**

    Promotional Material.. 191
    Follow-Up Contacts 192

PART IV— **NONHOSPITAL PHYSICIAN RECRUITMENT**.........**193**

Chapter 16— **Recruitment for a Private Practice** **195**

    Development Phase.. 195
    Implementation Phase 196

Chapter 17— **Recruitment for Health Maintenance Organizations** **199**
            HMO Models 199
            Recruiting Considerations 201

Epilogue **207**

Appendix A— Case Study of an External Physician Recruitment **209**

Index **213**

Preface

Physician recruitment as an organized effort has been overlooked until recently by health care professionals. In the past, hospital administrators relied on continued support from their medical staff and reacted only to changes as they occurred. Administrators generally did not take action in anticipation of changes in their hospital's medical staff for fear of disrupting existing referral patterns. The health care field has changed significantly in the last decade, however, and nowhere has this change been more apparent than in the area of physician recruitment. Today, in order to provide quality health care and maintain a viable institution, administration must attract and retain medical staff that is supportive of the hospital.

Over the past several years, many hospitals have experienced changing medical staff affiliations. Some hospitals have lost physicians to other hospitals in the same area, while others have lost physicians to other parts of the country. Whatever the reason, if a hospital is experiencing a declining census, it must consider the possibility of structuring a physician recruitment program that will attract new physicians so that existing levels of health care can be increased to meet future demands of the community.

In a more recent development, surveys have suggested that an oversupply of physicians can be anticipated during the next 10 years. If this is the case, it is more important than ever before to formulate a physician recruitment program. This program should be compatible with each facility's long-range planning goals; it should anticipate the services to be offered and thus the mix of physicians that will be needed. If hospitals do not adopt such proactive philosophies but react instead only to existing patterns and trends regarding physician staffing, it is doubtful whether their goals will be met and the desirable level of quality care attained.

The intent of this handbook is to provide a step-by-step approach for developing a successful physician recruitment program, whether to reverse the trend of a declining census or to plan for future growth.

Suzanne McNeely Lewitt
July 1982

Acknowledgments

We are grateful to Donna Friedman and Leora Udkoff for their valuable contributions to this book.

Donna Friedman holds a master's degree from the UCLA School of Public Health, with specialization in health services and hospital administration. Her background includes administration of the International Ladies Garment Workers Union Health Center in New York and service as director of professional relations for Medical Career Services (MCS).

Leora Udkoff has a Masters of Science degree in health services administration from UCLA. She has worked as an administrative analyst with Hyatt Medical Enterprises Inc. for the past three years. Her work there has been concentrated in the areas of planning, marketing, finance, and quality assurance. She has also worked with Medical Career Services (MCS) in developing hospital recruitment programs.

Part I

Development of the Physician Recruitment Process

In the first six chapters we outline the development phases of the physician recruitment process. The process begins with the preparation of a strategic plan and the establishment of a planning committee. Based on these initial steps, the process encompasses a physician need analysis, an indepth market analysis, a choice of recruitment program options that best serve the hospital and the community, decisions as to the use of recruitment firms, and, finally, a determination of financial and budgetary factors that will guide the recruitment process.

Chapter 1

Marketing Strategy and the Planning Committee

Is your hospital's census declining? Are other hospitals in your area drawing potential patients away from your facility? Is another hospital attracting your hospital's chief admitting physicians? Is your hospital experiencing extreme financial difficulty due to a decrease in overall activity?

Is your hospital considering the addition of specialized services in the future, thereby necessitating a specialty physician not currently practicing in your community? Is your hospital losing physician referrals because another hospital in the service area is offering new medical equipment and extra amenities, such as private rooms, gourmet meals, and cable television? Is the director of your hospital's emergency room planning on leaving in the next two months? Are you concerned about your hospital's future position in the community as the health care environment changes?

If, with respect to your facility, the answer to any of these questions is yes, it may be profitable for you to utilize marketing as a recruiting tool, both to encourage physicians to locate to your community and to strategically market your hospital to physicians within the community. Marketing is a method that can increase hospital utilization and improve the hospital's total posture within the medical community.

THE MARKETING PROCESS

Why do we refer to physician recruitment as a marketing process? Physician recruitment follows the marketing definition of the right *product* in the right *place* at the right *price* with the right *promotion*. In the case of physician recruitment, the physician represents the market. The *product* is the potential practice you are presenting to the physician. The *place* is your facility and community. The price is a combination of the cost of your recruitment program and the salary or financial arrangement provided to the physician. Finally, the *promotion* is the recruitment effort undertaken by the administrator, medical staff, and governing board to sell the product to the market, that is, to the physician.[1]

In order to develop a successful physician recruiting program through marketing, a strategic plan is necessary. The organization of the program should be based on a carefully designed planning methodology. Typically, the planning sequence will include the specification of objectives, the development of strategies to achieve the objectives, implementation of the strategies, and, finally, feedback and evaluation to modify or adjust current strategies and implementation procedures.[2]

These planning elements can be applied to physician recruitment in the following ways:

- The specification of objectives for physician recruitment is done by a planning committee, which determines the need for physicians and then analyzes the market's environment, problems, and opportunities.
- Once the objectives have been determined, they can be translated into operational terms by a recruitment committee. This committee is responsible for the development of strategies and the implementation of the physician recruitment program.
- Feedback and evaluation of the program are essential parts of the ongoing recruitment process.
- Follow-up and retention of the recruited physicians are vital monitoring functions to ensure the success of the recruitment program.

The above sequence outlines both development and implementation. Development includes the planning function, while the implementation phase is concerned with the successful execution of the physician recruitment program.

ESTABLISHING THE PLANNING COMMITTEE

The development phase of the recruitment program begins with the organization of a planning committee. This committee should include the administrator, a governing board member, a medical staff member, and other professional staff support.

The planning committee is responsible for laying the groundwork to coordinate the recruitment process. This groundwork involves determining physician need, conducting a market analysis, choosing between recruitment program options, deciding if a recruitment firm will be utilized, and considering financial commitments and arrangements. The administrator should assign these responsibilities to the members of the planning committee.

The planning committee is also responsible for deciding which method of recruitment will be utilized—external or internal. With external recruitment, the hospital recruits physicians from outside the available physician resources in the community. This involves identifying interested physician candidates, prescreening, interviewing, arranging for on-site visits, and performing follow-up activities. Internal recruitment takes place within the immediate medical community. Retention of the active medical staff of the hospital is an integral part of the internal recruitment process and should be an ongoing concern of the hospital administrator. If there are physicians on staff at the hospital who are inactive or are tapering down their admissions, internal recruitment can become a valuable tool that the administrator can use to increase admissions. This process can encompass a variety of techniques directed toward increasing physician activity at the hospital.

NOTES

1. Don I. Snook, Jr., "Marketing Strategies" (Paper delivered at American Hospital Association seminars, Miami, San Antonio, Chicago, 1981), pp. 1–5.

2. Eric Berkowitz and William A. Flexner, "The Marketing Audit: A Tool for Health Service Organizations," *Health Care Management Review* 3, no. 4 (Fall 1978): 51–57.

Chapter 2

Determining the Need for Physicians

One of the most important functions of the planning committee is to perform a physician need analysis. This is a basic function in the physician recruitment process. It is, however, often performed rapidly and without consideration of the myriad of possibilities and ramifications of the physician recruitment program. The key to developing an effective program is for the planning committee to give prior thought to and to research the need for the recruitment effort. If the planning committee addresses this function in a coordinated, systematic way, unnecessary steps and the wasting of time can be avoided.

Historically, hospitals and other health care institutions have expected community physicians to support their facilities faithfully with a continuing flow of patient referrals. Hospitals rarely developed a comprehensive program of encouraging physicians to utilize the hospital; even more rarely did they develop programs to attract new physicians to the hospital medical staff.

Today, however, when a hospital census begins to drop, warning lights should flash in the administrative offices. Why is the census dropping? Is it due to a shortage of physician referrals, to faulty data, or to a seasonal fluctuation?

These questions can be answered by analyzing physician need in the community. This analysis should be both quantitative and qualitative. The quantitative analysis should be based on statistical information relating to population needs and manpower availability. The qualitative study should address all the issues not related to a statistical objective/needs analysis—the special makeup of the hospital and the concerns of the medical staff, the hospital's governing board, and the community. All of these factors must be evaluated before it can be determined what the need is for physicians in the community. The planning committee should assign the task of gathering and organizing these data to those individuals who are best suited to do the job.

The following techniques for determining physician need involve a coordination of quantitative and qualitative studies as parts of a complete physician analysis.

QUANTITATIVE ANALYSIS

Physician Surplus

In the past few years, many different studies have analyzed the physician supply/demand situation in the United States.[1] For example, a study by the Bureau of Health Professions (BHP) shows projections for 1990 that do not necessarily add up to a surplus of any significant size. However, the Congress's Office of Technology Assessment has issued a critique of the BHP numbers noting that a change of just one assumption of the study would yield a surplus of 185,000 M.D.'s.

The most recent manpower study, published in September 1980, was prepared by the Graduate Medical Education National Advisory Committee (GMENAC).[2] This federally funded task force, composed primarily of physicians, concluded that:

- There will be 70,000 more physicians than required in 1990.
- Most specialties will have a surplus.
- Some specialties will be in balance, including the primary care fields of osteopathic general practice, family practice, general internal medicine, and general pediatrics.
- Shortages will be experienced in psychiatry, physical medicine and rehabilitation, and emergency medicine.
- Valid criteria for designating geographic areas as adequately served or underserved have not been developed.

According to the GMENAC study, the factors contributing to the impending surplus in 1990 are the increase in the entering class size of U.S. allopathic and osteopathic medical schools from 8 to 19,000 over the past 14 years, the yearly influx into practice of 3 to 4,000 alien and U.S. citizen graduates of foreign medical schools, and the steadily rising numbers of medical visits cared for by nurse practitioners, physician assistants and nurse-midwives.

The GMENAC study recommends the following: a 17 percent decrease in U.S. medical school enrollment compared to current levels; sharp restrictions into the United States of students from foreign medical schools; no further rise in the number of nonphysician health care providers being trained; and prompt adjustments in the number of residency training positions in individual specialties to bring supply into balance with requirements in the 1990s.

Other GMENAC recommendations relate to the desirability of increasing the number of minority students in medical schools, the urgent need to develop criteria for assessing the adequacy of health services in small geographic areas, initiatives to improve the geographic distribution of physicians, programs to emphasize ambulatory care and training, and new professional service reimbursement plans to help achieve health policy objectives.

If an oversupply of physicians develops, the health care field should utilize need data to develop planning methodologies. This will enable a hospital to select the most appropriate physician mix compatible with its long-range planning goals.

Clearly, the physician supply problem is a controversial subject that must be carefully weighed and considered when analyzing present and future physician needs in a particular community. In this context, the information provided by the GMENAC study can be a useful tool in relating the numbers of physicians to population figures in a given area.

Physician/Population Ratios

Physician/population ratios are important indicators of the numbers and kinds of physicians available. A reference book published by the American Medical Association (AMA), *Physician Distribution and Medical Licensure in the United States,* shows the number of physicians, by specialty, for each state in the country.[3] By using a conversion formula, one can determine the physician/population ratio, that is, the number of physicians per 100,000 population by specialty. The method of conversion is as follows:

$$\frac{\text{Total number of physicians per specialty}}{\text{Total population}} = \frac{X}{100,000} \quad \frac{\text{(Number of physicians)}}{\text{(Per 100,000 population)}}$$

In the GMENAC study, 1978 figures on physician supply were used.[4] These figures have been converted into physician/population ratios and are listed in Table 2-1. The GMENAC study's projections of the corresponding figures for physician supply and the number of physicians required in 1990 are shown for comparative purposes and have also been converted into physician/population ratios.[5] These comparative data enable a health care institution to determine how many physicians are necessary per 100,000 population and which specialties will exhibit a surplus, or shortage, by 1990.

Table 2-1 Supply/Requirements of Physicians by Specialty: 1978 and Estimates for 1990

	M.D.'s per 100,000 Population			
	1978	1990		
Specialty	Supply	Supply	Requirement	Surplus (Shortage)
Primary Care				
General/Family practice	24.9	26.5	25.2	X
Internal medicine	22.6	30.2	29.0	X
Osteopathic general practice	6.2	9.8	9.3	X
Pediatrics	10.9	15.5	12.4	X
Total	64.6	82.1	75.9	X
Medical Specialties				
Allergy and immunology	1.0	1.3	1.0	X
Cardiology	3.5	6.1	3.2	X
Dermatology	2.3	3.0	3.0	
Gastroenterology	1.3	2.8	2.7	X
Hematology/Oncology	1.4	3.4	3.7	(X)
Pulmonary disease	1.3	2.9	1.5	X
Total	10.8	19.5	15.1	X
Surgical Specialties				
General surgery	14.0	14.5	9.7	X
Neurosurgery	1.4	2.1	1.0	X
OB/GYN	10.6	14.2	9.9	X
Ophthalmology	5.4	6.7	4.8	X
Orthopedic surgery	5.7	8.3	6.2	X
Otolaryngology	2.8	3.5	3.3	X
Plastic surgery	1.2	1.6	1.0	X
Thoracic surgery	1.0	1.2	1.0	X
Urology	3.3	3.8	3.2	X
Total	45.4	55.9	40.1	X
Other Specialties				
Anesthesiology	6.8	8.0	8.6	(X)
Child psychiatry	1.4	1.7	3.7	(X)
Emergency medicine	2.3	3.8	5.6	(X)
Neurology	2.2	3.6	2.3	X
Pathology	5.8	6.9	5.6	X
Preventive medicine	2.8	2.3	3.0	(X)
Psychiatry	11.5	12.5	15.8	(X)

Table 2-1 continued

| | M.D.'s per 100,000 Population | | | |
| | 1978 | 1990 | | |
Specialty	Supply	Supply	Require- ment	Surplus (Shortage)
Radiology	8.5	11.4	7.4	X
All other and unspecified	9.3	12.3	8.3	X
Total	50.6	62.5	60.3	X
Total Physicians	171.4	220.0	191.4	X

Note: Not all specialties are listed here, since some data were not available for comparison.

Source: U.S., Department of Health and Human Services, *Graduate Medical Education National Advisory Committee (GMENAC) Summary Report* (Washington, D.C.: U.S. Government Printing Office, 1980). 1990 population estimate: 243,513,000.

The table indicates that in 1978 the nation had a supply of 64.6 primary care physicians, 10.8 medical specialty physicians, 45.4 surgical specialty physicians, and 50.6 other specialty physicians per 100,000 population. These ratios are projected to increase in each major category to show a surplus of physicians by 1990. Only a few specialties are projected to be in short supply by 1990: hematology, oncology, anesthesiology, child psychiatry, emergency medicine, preventive medicine, and psychiatry.

One can relate this information to a specific area by analyzing the number of physicians by specialty that are located in the community. These numbers are available by county and state in *Physician Distribution and Medical Licensure.*

Once the ratios of area physicians to population have been determined, they can be compared to the required rates for relative need in 1990. If an area has 12 general/family practitioners for every 100,000 population and the required 1990 rate should be 25.2 general/family practitioners, it is reasonable to conclude that the area exhibits an undersupply of this type of physician and that recruitment should be considered.

Primary Care Visit Ratios

Another method for projecting physician need is to calculate primary care visit/demand ratios.[6] It has been estimated that an individual person will make an average of 2.6 primary care visits per year or from 2.0 to 3.5 physician visits (all types) per year in any given population.[7] Thus, in an area with a population of 10,000, there will be an average demand of 26,000 primary care visits or a demand range of 20,000 to 35,000 visits per year. How can this demand be translated to physician need?

One way to do this is to estimate physician productivity.[8] The average primary care physician sees an average of 25 patients per day. Physicians in new practices will usually work a five-day week, year round, with a vacation of four weeks. Thus, 48 weeks × 5 days × 25 visits = 6,000 visits per year, which can be used as an estimate of a new physician's productivity.

A physician who has been working in an established practice situation will probably work less, possibly a four-day week with six weeks vacation each year. In this case, 46 weeks × 4 days × 25 visits = 4,600 visits per year. This figure can be used as an estimate of an established physician's productivity.

After identifying productivity estimates, the next step is to calculate the productivity/demand ratio. For example, if the projected need for new physicians equates to 26,000 visits/year* divided by 6,000 visits/physician/year, the productivity/demand ratio is 4.3 physicians for a population of 10,000.

Both of these techniques for determining need—physician-population ratios and primary care visit ratios—are useful quantitative tools that can be utilized by a hospital.

Patient Age Analysis

Another way of computing physician need is to estimate demand by age of patients. This requires access to area population figures, broken down by age and sex. If such information is attainable, one can apply estimates of patient need for physician visits to population figures. The estimates of patient need to physician visits can be determined by reviewing the actual demand for physician visits in 1978, as shown in Table 2–2.

Using the data in this table, one can compare the number of people in the population to the demand for physician visits. This in turn can be applied to the number of physicians available (using the figure of 6,000 visits for new physicians and 4,600 visits for established physicians).

Table 2-2 Number of Physician Visits per Person in the United States, 1978

Type of Visit	All Ages	Under 17 Years	17–24 Years	25–44 Years	45–64 Years	65 Years and Over
Physician visits						
Both sexes	4.8	4.1	4.3	4.7	5.3	6.3
Male	4.0	4.2	3.0	3.4	4.7	5.8
Female	5.4	4.0	5.5	5.8	5.9	6.6

Source: U.S., Department of Health, Education, and Welfare, National Center for Health Statistics, Current Estimates from the Health Interview Survey: United States, 1978. (Washington, D.C.: U.S. Government Printing Office, 1978).

---

*Using an average of 2.6 primary care visits × 10,000 population = 26,000 visits per year.

Manpower Studies

Manpower availability should be analyzed through an indepth study of the medical staff at the hospital and other physicians in the community. With this information at hand, a study of the community in general can help to develop the most efficient program for physician recruitment. This study should address the following three areas:

1. Hospital analysis
    * yearly patient admissions/physician
    * yearly patient admissions/physician by age and specialty

    * yearly patient admissions/physician by office location
    * physician's last admission to the hospital
    * revenues generated per physician
    * market share

2. Community physician analysis
    * population by physician and specialty
    * number of physicians by age, specialty, and primary hospital affiliation
    * physicians by office location
    * referral patterns

3. Community analysis
    * available medical services in area
    * medical services the population needs or wants
    * recruited physician characteristics
    * population's ethnic, religious, educational, and age background
    * population's mobility
    * community's ability to pay for services rendered

The above list is applied as a reference guide for each of the three study areas—hospital analysis, community physician analysis, and community analysis—discussed in the following paragraphs. Many of these factors will also be incorporated into the marketing analysis presented in the following chapter.

Hospital Analysis

Yearly Patient Admissions/Physician. This ratio is a measure of a physician's productivity at a hospital. It relates the number of patients admitted during the past 12-month period to each physician on the medical staff. The average number of patients per month should also be calculated as a monthly comparison of productivity.

Yearly Patient Admissions/Physician by Age and Specialty. This ratio is a measure of the number of patients admitted to the hospital during a 12-month period, correlated with the physician's age and specialty. By analyzing the age of the physicians who admitted the most, one can readily see if a potential problem will arise as these physicians ease off their practices as they get older. If the specialists perceived as critical to the hospital are not currently admitting a significant number of patients, efforts should be made toward encouraging an increase in admission patterns. If this is not possible, external recruitment should be considered.

Yearly Patient Admissions/Physician by Office Location. An analysis of which physicians are admitting and their office locations will enable one to decide if distance is a factor affecting the hospital's admissions. Perhaps by encouraging physicians to relocate their offices or by building a new medical building close to the hospital, the incentive needed to increase admissions can be developed.

Physician's Last Admission to the Hospital. It is useful to know which physicians are currently strong supporters of the hospital and which have not been admitting on a regular basis. It is then easier to pinpoint the physicians who need encouragement by the administration to facilitate a better admission record.

Revenues Generated per Physician. The hospital dollar revenues generated by each physician range widely by specialty and individual physician practices. Because this ratio is an important measure of physician productivity, it should be analyzed on a continual basis.

Market Share. It is very important to analyze the market share that the hospital has in relation to the other hospitals in the area. Market share refers to what proportion of the patients available in the community are coming to the hospital. If the hospital has a low census in pediatric patients and a competing facility across town is absorbing the majority of this population segment, one should analyze what is occurring at present in this service. Are the pediatricians on staff at the hospital admitting all their patients to the facility, or is most of their activity at the competing hospital? Are the pediatricians getting older, resulting in their activity decreasing overall? The reasons for the hospital's low market share in this specific service should be determined by consulting the staff physicians. If an increase cannot be obtained with the existing medical staff, the recruitment of a new physician should be anticipated.

Market share data involving competing hospitals may be difficult to obtain. If a particular hospital is reluctant to release this information, other potential sources may be the area health systems agency or the planning office of the state department of health.

Community Physician Analysis

Population by Physician and Specialty. By analyzing the population/physician ratios, it is possible to ascertain if the community requires more physicians or merely a greater percentage of utilization by the present physicians in the community.

Number of Physicians by Age, Specialty, and Primary Hospital Affiliation. This study will pinpoint a shortage or surplus of a given specialty and profile the average age of the community's physicians. It is also useful to know the hospital affiliation for reference purposes. This information is valuable for planning purposes and is also of great interest to an incoming physician.

Physicians by Office Location. If the majority of physicians' offices are located adjacent to the hospital, yet few of the physicians are actively admitting, each of the physicians should be contacted and encouraged to make greater use of the hospital's services. Are the majority of the physicians located in one area at a greater distance from the hospital? Would new office buildings at a reduced rent be of interest to these practitioners? Perhaps the physicians are widely dispersed throughout the community. If so, is it possible to encourage them to relocate closer to the hospital? Presumably, closer proximity to the hospital would lead to greater utilization, in terms of greater convenience for the patients as well as the physicians.

Referral Patterns. It is extremely important to review the referral patterns of the physicians at the facility. Are they referring their patients to heavy admitters of the facility, or are these referrals going to physicians outside of the existing medical staff? Encouraging the medical staff to refer to physicians who are affiliated with the hospital will increase the hospital's census rather than a competing facility's census.

Community Analysis

Available Medical Services in the Area. A careful study must be conducted of the services that are currently available to the community. If the hospital is planning on adding a cardiologist and a cardiac care unit, will there be a need for this service or will there be a duplication in neighborhood services? Is there a neonatal care center or burn ward? The other health care resources in the service area should be analyzed first to negate the possibility of overlap and duplication. A needs assessment analysis might identify a service that is presently missing but is needed in the community and thus lead to its future provision at the hospital.

Medical Services the Population Needs or Desires. Is there a need for an alcohol detoxification center? Does the community want a family practice clinic? Does the medical staff express a need for a specific specialty? By answering these questions first, one can save a lot of unnecessary work and time and ultimately provide a truly desired service.

Recruited Physician Characteristics. Familiarization with the community and realistic expectations are prerequisites for a successful recruitment program. Would a foreign medical graduate, a doctor of osteopathy, a minority or a woman physician be acceptable in the community? These questions should be explored along with those tailored specifically to the hospital and must be answered honestly within the context of the community's profile. Specific considerations regarding foreign medical graduates and doctors of osteopathy are discussed in Chapter 8.

Population's Ethnic, Religious, Educational, and Age Background. Different population characteristics can have a pronounced effect on the physician need of a community. If the population is young and of childbearing years, the needs will be different compared to those of a community composed of mostly elderly individuals. If the community has a large minority population, it might be wise to recruit a minority physician. The same principle applies to religious and ethnic populations. The community should be surveyed in detail so that the physician best suited to the area will be selected.

Population's Mobility. Does the community have a transient or stable population? Is there a seasonal influx of outside individuals into the area that places an additional stress on the existing services? Another important factor to consider is the growth of the area population over the years. Is the area exhibiting a rapid population growth? What segments of the population are increasing? Are the children increasing at a faster rate than the elderly, or is the community growing in age with the youth leaving for other places? Such population changes can place demands on specific health care services and physician specialties and should therefore be monitored. These trends will also have a bearing on recruitment decisions and should be studied prior to making commitments to a specific physician specialty.

Community's Ability to Pay for Services Rendered. It is important to analyze the economic situation of the people who utilize the hospital's services. If the hospital decides to establish a family planning clinic and recruits a physician to administer the program without taking into account the fact that the population is indigent and cannot afford to pay for the services, a great deal of money and time will be wasted. In a more affluent community, there would probably be a greater demand for specialty physicians such as plastic surgeons, dermatologists, and psychiatrists. Yet the latter two specialties produce few admissions, a factor that should be considered in the physician recruitment formula for the particular hospital.

Summary

In short, the quantitative techniques available to a hospital in determining physician need are:

- physician surplus analysis
- physician/population ratios
- primary care visit ratios (physician productivity and productivity/demands)
- patient age analysis
- manpower availability (hospital, community physician, and community) analyses

The data required for each of the analyses we have examined can be gathered from hospital records and in contacts with local health systems agencies. Once the rates and data are available, realistic conclusions can be reached bridging the desires of the community, the hospital medical staff, and the administration with actual health care needs. Each hospital will have its own particular questions and data requirements relating to the surrounding area. The types of analyses we have described will assist the hospital to develop a strong base upon which to build a successful recruitment program.

QUALITATIVE ANALYSIS

Statistical data gathered through a community and hospital analysis are critical in developing a successful recruitment program. It should not, however, be the sole indicator of physician need. Statistics alone do not always take into account the qualitative factors which are the particular and/or unique characteristics of the community, hospital, medical staff and patterns of health care delivery. A hospital, in order to develop a comprehensive physician recruitment program, should undertake a qualitative analysis concurrently with the quantitative study.

Community Information

When examining the community, the administrator should look for previous medical trends, distinctive population traits, geographic limitations and other distinguishing features. For example, simple population statistics of a community may indicate an adequate supply of internists. Because of the unique geography of the community, however, a high incidence of respiratory cases may occur. Additional internists therefore would be required, although the population statistics alone do not suggest this.

Hospital Data

A hospital must also be considered in a qualitative study. As we have seen, by examining hospital statistics the administrator can focus on the areas of greatest need. Again, it should be stressed that since statistics are not the complete indicator of physician need, other hospital factors must be considered in conjunction with the data. The statistics may demonstrate a need for a specialist; however, due to a lack of specialized hospital facilities and/or resources, this might prove impractical. The hospital's financial and physical condition then becomes an overriding concern. Since the physicians do not work in a vacuum and the hospital is of such focal importance, all hospital factors that impact on a physician recruitment program should be examined.

Medical Staff Concerns

Although the hospital's influence is critical, the medical staff holds the real key to a successful recruitment program. By contacting the physicians directly, the administrator can discover which physicians are sympathetic to the recruitment efforts and, more importantly, if there is any resentment or objection. This early, forthright approach will one hopes curtail opposition.

It is important to emphasize that there will rarely be a consensus of opinion on physician needs between the medical staff and other hospital personnel. It is the role of the administrator to analyze the perceptions of the medical staff in order to determine the qualitative physician needs of the hospital and community.

Patterns of Health Care Delivery

The patterns of care in a community also will determine a recruitment program. If patients are seeking care elsewhere because they cannot locate a particular specialty or must wait weeks for an appointment, a physician need is indicated. If the statistics indicate an adequate number of primary care physicians, yet some of the staff physicians perceive a need for at least two more family physicians for referral purposes, a need once again is indicated.

The switchboard calls coming into the hospital can be monitored to determine those that are demanding a particular specialty and those that are being referred elsewhere. Another technique for reviewing referral patterns is to keep track of those patients who enter the system through the emergency room without physicians and to determine where these patients are ultimately treated. Follow-up on patient movement can help to determine in which specialty or specialties the hospital is experiencing the greatest loss in patients and, therefore, in revenue.

It can be seen that a quantitative study alone does not provide the complete picture necessary for a comprehensive physician recruitment effort. By combining a qualitative analysis of the community, hospital, medical staff, and patterns of health care, the opportunities for a successful program are greatly enhanced.

NOTES

1. Marian Kircher, "Doctor Surplus—What Will 1990 Look Like?" *Medical Economics,* September 29, 1980, p. 54.

2. U.S., Department of Health and Human Services, *Graduate Medical Education National Advisory Committee (GMENAC) Summary Report* (Washington, D.C.: U.S. Government Printing Office, 1980), pp. 3–27.

3. American Medical Association, *Physician Distribution and Medical Licensure in the United States* (Monroe, Wis: American Medical Association, 1978), pp. 91–146.

4. Health and Human Services, *GMENAC Report,* p. 11.

5. Ibid., p. 14.

6. Don Black, "Steps to Successful Recruitment" (Paper delivered at American Hospital Association seminars, Miami, San Antonio, Chicago, 1981), pp. 1–16.

7. U.S., Department of Health, Education, and Welfare, *Advanced Data—1979 Summary, Vital Health Statistics of the National Center for Health Statistics* (Washington, D.C.: National Center for Health Statistics, 1979), p. 1.

8. Arthur Owens, "Doctor Surplus—Where Things Stand Now," *Medical Economics,* September 29, 1980, p. 64.

Chapter 3

Market Analysis

After the planning committee has completed the physician need analysis, an indepth market analysis should be conducted. This analysis should focus on the environment, the factors that give rise to potential marketing problems, and the opportunities that surround the available practice situation.

The hospital administrator is usually the originator of the market analysis. The administrator should seek the assistance of professional and medical staff in developing a complete review of the environment, potential problems, and opportunities.

ENVIRONMENT

The successful recruitment of a physician by a hospital is dependent on the atmosphere of the potential practice situation. What is the environment like? Will it meet the needs of the physician and the physician's family? A thorough study of the environment and its impact upon a physician should include treatment of the demographic factors described in the following paragraphs.[1]

Service Area

The geographical area served by the hospital should be analyzed in terms of location, climate, cultural amenities, and education. What can the area offer to a physician and the physician's family? Are there good schools in the vicinity? What kind of cultural activities are available, either nearby or within the community? Are there convenient shopping centers nearby? In all cases, it is important to consider geographical preferences when selecting recruitment candidates. If a physician dislikes water sports and loves snow skiing, it will be difficult to recruit him for a beach community.

Population

All aspects of the service area population should be considered, taking into account the aggregate number of people, the range in ages, the number of people in each age group, local environmental influences on health, and data on morbidity, mortality, and births. These data can indicate what types of physicians should be recruited. Population data can provide a comprehensive picture of what the community is like and what kind of patients a recruited physician would be serving in the community.

Neighborhood Economics

The immediate neighborhood of the hospital should be examined to identify socioeconomic influences on local health care needs. Primary contributors to the local economy and the sources of third party payments to physicians should also be studied. These factors can impact upon recruitment and can be important influences on a physician's decision to locate in a community. It is also useful to determine if the physician has any preferences as to patient types. Some physicians prefer blue-collar workers as patients because they seem more appreciative and less likely to challenge a physician's decisions.

Health Manpower Availability

The area should be analyzed indepth in terms of number of physicians, types of specialties, ages of physicians, and available ancillary health care personnel. These data will suggest the type of physician that should be recruited. They will also indicate to a potential physician recruit what kind of competition can be anticipated from other physicians and what referral patterns are available in the area. For example, an orthopedic surgeon might not be willing to relocate to an area that already has an oversupply of orthopedic surgeons.

Nursing Availability

Due to the chronic shortage of nurses in most areas of the United States, nursing availability is a crucial factor to be considered by incoming physicians. The quantity and quality of nurses in a community are often the first things a physician considers when contemplating relocation.

Because of the importance of the nursing issue, the hospital may be well-advised to develop a nursing recruitment program concurrently with the physician recruitment program. This will demonstrate to the physician that the hospital is actively attempting to recruit additional nurses to meet the needs of the newly recruited physician. In this sense, nurse recruitment is an integral part of a market analysis and an important factor in recruiting physicians.

Utilization of Health Services

Utilization data on the community and hospital should be compared with similar information from other health care facilities. It should be determined which diseases are causing local residents to be hospitalized, which institutions the residents are using, and in what numbers. This will facilitate the development of better ways to serve the hospital's current patients and to increase the hospital's share of the caseload.

One factor that will affect a hospital's utilization is its proximity to another hospital. Are there several hospitals in the area that have low census patient populations? Are there tertiary level (highly comprehensive) facilities nearby in case a patient needs to be transferred for specialized services? All of these factors can impact upon the type of practice available for a prospective physician.

Politics

A major determiner of costs and benefits in health care is the political establishment, at the local, state, or national level. Politics have indeed impacted upon the health planning area (e.g., certificates of need, the Hill-Burton program, health systems agencies), making public funds available along with regulations to be followed. As the hospital develops its physician recruitment marketing strategy, it must take into consideration planning and reimbursement guidelines and new legislation.

An example of important legislation that raised questions regarding physician recruitment efforts is the Medicare and Medicaid Antifraud and Abuse Amendments to PL 95–142 (1977).[2] These amendments provided specific penalties for transgressions against Medicare or Medicaid programs for certain practices that have long been regarded by professional organizations as unethical. These amendments raised questions regarding the offering of guaranteed incomes, free or discounted office space, and the financing of office expenses, as part of a physician recruitment program because these inducements could be in violation of the law. In addition, violation of these amendments can negatively impact upon the reimbursement a hospital receives from the government, causing the reduction or withholding of potentially reimbursable dollars.

The Department of Health and Human Services (formerly the Department of Health, Education, and Welfare) has since clarified the law, stating that a hospital would be in violation if it explicitly promised a physician patient referrals, offered kickbacks, or based other benefits on the volume or number of admissions a physician contributed to a hospital.[3] (Techniques for developing appropriate contractual agreements between the hospital and a newly recruited physician are described in Chapter 6.)

Technology

New strides in technology are causing dramatic changes in the health care field, creating new clients, professionals, and services that can impact upon a hospital. For example, a CAT scanner is a highly complex diagnostic tool that has become important in the health care field. Indeed, sophisticated equipment like the CAT scanner can serve as a strong recruiting tool. If such equipment is not available and a physician recruit requires this type of equipment, it might be important to consider procuring it, taking into account the need for government approval and the projected revenues and expenses in operating the new equipment.

MARKETING PROBLEMS

Several general problems may arise in the marketing environment and affect the physician recruitment process.[4] These problems are briefly described in the following paragraphs.

Negative Market

A negative market occurs when, for whatever reason, a product is avoided by potential consumers. For example, in the health care field, a staff relationship may be perceived as negative by the physician due to conflicting affiliations with the hospital, or the hospital may have a poor reputation due to an incompetent medical staff or weak administration, or the hospital may be located in an unsafe area. Clearly, if the hospital wishes to recruit a physician in this type of negative market, its administration and planning committee must address the specific problems that are hindering the recruitment effort.

Inert Market

An inert market is similar to a negative market in that no activity is taking place. The difference is that the inert market has more potential for improvement. Some factors that can cause inertia in recruiting a physician are inconvenient hours, lack of parking spaces, an inefficient receptionist or admitting office, and weak community relations. Adjustments in these areas by the administration can improve the prospects for physician recruitment.

Engaged Market

An engaged market is one that is involved with competitive organizations. The engaged market is common in the health care field, since physicians are usually affiliated with more than one hospital. In an engaged market, a major question is how to encourage a physician to be a more active admitter. (Medical staff retention and utilization techniques are discussed in Chapters 14 and 15 in the context of internal recruitment.)

Unrealized Market

An unrealized market is a situation in which desired relationships are not taking place due to undetermined demand. An example of such a market is a recently graduated resident who is looking for a community that in turn, is actively seeking a physician. In this case, the hospital and community should analyze the physicians available in the immediate area. A teaching hospital closest to the facility would be a natural source for this type of market. A resident who is already affiliated with the community would be much more likely to enjoy a practice there than one who is affiliated with a hospital 3,000 miles away. (Techniques for analyzing the residency market are examined in a subsequent chapter.)

Another unrealized market worth pursuing is a physician in a community who is dissatisfied with the present practice situation. Is it possible to capitalize on this physician's dissatisfaction and encourage a move to a different hospital? An effective internal recruitment technique would be for the existing medical staff to scan the physician community for individuals who could be recruited to the facility.

Declining Market

A declining market is one in which a diminishing number of relationships appears likely to continue to decline in the future. A decrease in the number and utilization of physicians on staff is a common worry of hospital administrators. The hospital must be aware of a declining level of physician interaction that becomes a problem and of the probability that such a decline will continue unless specifically addressed.

One way to analyze this type of market is to monitor the ages and activities of the present medical staff. As the hospital's physicians age, it becomes increasingly important to recruit younger physicians to the medical staff. If the hospital shows a decrease in census, the recruitment of new staff members will help to increase its potential activity. (A sample active physician profile is presented in Chapter 14.)

Undesired Market

An undesired market is one in which supply exceeds demand. The most common type of undesired market is the situation in which there is an oversupply of specialist physicians in the community. This problem is magnified in the larger cities, where many physicians tend to congregate. Other examples of undesired markets are an overload of surgeons compared to operating room facilities or an oversupply of foreign medical graduates (FMGs) in an area that wants only American-trained physicians.

Fluctuating Market

A fluctuating market is one in which the supply of physicians is changing inconsistently with the demand for medical services. The numbers and availability of physicians in the community are not shifting in line with the demand generated in the area, or a specific specialty group on staff at the hospital, such as surgeons, may all take vacation or attend conventions at a time when demand for their services is at the highest level. This type of fluctuation in supply and demand should be monitored continuously. An effective strategy to deal with these types of changes would be to educate the medical staff on the importance of coordinating seasonal variations in census trends with physician practice patterns.

OPPORTUNITIES

In order to determine the potential opportunities that a hospital and community can provide to an incoming physician, a coordinated analysis of the *needs, attitudes,* and *motivation* of the physician in relation to the hospital and community is necessary.[5] Need can be viewed as the condition suggesting or requiring a physician to relocate to an area. Attitudes reflect the desire of the physician to act. Motivation is the impetus that will persuade a potential candidate to become a staff physician.

Need

Responsive hospitals and administrators are highly concerned with the needs and wants of their medical staff and patients. A conceptual problem arises, however, in that need is not a well-defined term. In popular parlance, it is used interchangeably with such terms as *want, desire,* and *demand.*[6] In relation to physician recruitment, need can also refer to those elements necessary for the physician to set up practice. If a physician has professional needs, such as certain highly technological equipment to practice a specialty, it is important to determine that that equipment is part of the physician's requirements for beginning a practice, if the cost factor is appropriate.

Personal needs of a potential physician recruit are also important factors to consider in the recruitment process. What kind of family does the physician have? Does the physician have children who require schooling? Is the family involved in sports, and does the community offer these activities? What type of specialist referral patterns does the physician prefer? These are just a few of the need factors that can be translated into opportunities as the recruitment committee strategically presents the practice opportunity to the physician.

Attitudes

The attitudes of a physician and the physician's family about a potential move, the geographical location of the area, the weather, and the size of the community, hospital, and schools are all factors that the recruitment committee needs to be aware of when attempting to recruit a physician. It is of the utmost importance that the physician's attitudes and perceptions are understood. With this knowledge and understanding, the community and hospital can be best presented to satisfy the physician's needs and attitudes.

Motivation

The final step in facilitating the recruitment process is the translation of a potential recruit into a staff physician through provision of a specific stimulus. Such a motivational stimulus must be part of the initial recruitment effort, organized in such a way as to best meet the needs and attitudes of the physician and the physician's family. Another common motivating stimulus is the financial arrangement for the incoming physician, including benefits of free office space and/or secretarial assistance for the first six months or year of practice.

SUMMARY

The needs and attitudinal and motivating factors that determine where a physician would like to practice are important considerations in persuading a physician candidate to relocate in a given community. A combination of all these factors (needs, attitudes, and motivation) into a cohesive approach toward physician recruitment will heighten measurably the chances of bringing a physician candidate into a community.

In the recruitment effort, it is important to realize that, to be successful, it is necessary to recruit both the physician and the physician's spouse. If a physician is considering a practice opportunity, the financial arrangement is generous, and the medical staff is friendly, one might confidently expect the recruitment of the physician. However, if the physician's spouse is not happy with the area, the schools, the employment opportunities, the age group of the community, or the housing, the hospital's recruitment efforts might easily fail.

(In this connection, we must note that, in many instances throughout this book, the physician's spouse will be referred to as a wife. At this time, the majority of physicians in the United States are male. True, the dynamics of the medical industry are such that more and more females are graduating from medical schools across the country. However, in the majority of recruitment situations that we have encountered, the physician has been male and the spouse female. Accordingly, we will defer to the reality of the present-day situation in physician recruitment, on the clear understanding of course that we do not mean to imply thereby that there are no female physicians practicing medicine in the country or that the recruitment process will never include a female physician and her husband.)

In Exhibit 3–1, we present a sample market analysis, which translates the concepts discussed in this chapter into a format that allows the administrator to gather data about the community. Upon completion of the marketing analysis based on this format, the hospital should have gained a great deal of insight about the medical environment and the community. At this point, the hospital must become introspective and analyze its own capabilities as they relate to performance of the recruitment function.

Exhibit 3–1 Sample Market Analysis

A. *General Hospital Information*
  1. Name of hospital: _____
  2. Address of hospital: _____
  3. Telephone number: ( ) _____
  4. Form of ownership: _____
  5. Facility type: _____
  6. Number of beds: _____
  7. Personnel: Administrator _____
      Chief of medical staff _____
      Director of nursing _____
      Controller _____
      Chairman of the board _____

Exhibit 3-1 continued

8. *Services:*   *No. of beds, description*
   M/S   _____
   Peds   _____
   OB   _____
   Nursery   _____
   ICU   _____
   CCU   _____
   Emergency   _____
   Outpatient   _____
   Other   _____
   Other   _____
   TOTAL   _____
9. Occupancy rate: _____
10. Avg. daily census: _____
11. Patient mix—by payer source (Medicare, Medicaid, other):
   _____
   _____
   _____

B. *Community Profile*
   1. Service area land size: _____
   2. Population of service area: _____
      a. Age ranges: _____
      _____
      _____
      b. Area morbidity/mortality: _____
      _____
      _____
   3. Average income: _____
   4. Primary contributors to economy (major industry and employers):_____
      _____
      _____
      _____
   5. Cultural entertainment (sports, theatre, etc.): _____
      _____
      _____
   6. Climate: _____
   7. Nearest large city/airport transportation: _____
      _____

C. *Competitive Hospitals*
   1. Nearby hospitals:

Name	Distance	Lic.	Beds Planned	% Occupancy	Avg. Chg. PPD	Chief Admitters

Exhibit 3–1 continued

2. What services do the competitors offer that your hospital does not?

        Name of Facility   Service

_____

_____

_____

_____

3. What services does your facility offer that the above-mentioned hospitals do not? ___

_____

_____

_____

_____

_____

D. *Manpower Availability*

  1. Number of physicians in area: _____

2. By Specialty	M.D. Ratios (Per 100,000 pop.)	Required 1990 Rate*	Deficit
Primary Care			
General/family practice		25.2	
Internal medicine		29.0	
Osteopathic general practice		9.3	
Pediatrics		12.4	
Total		75.9	
Medical Specialists			
Allergy and immunology		1.0	
Cardiology		3.2	
Dermatology		3.0	
Gastroenterology		2.7	
Hematology/oncology		3.7	
Pulmonary disease		1.5	
Total		15.1	
Surgical Specialties			
General surgery		9.7	
Neurosurgery		1.0	
OB/GYN		9.9	
Ophthalmology		4.8	
Orthopedic surgery		6.2	
Otolaryngology		3.3	
Plastic surgery		1.0	
Thoracic surgery		1.0	
Urology		3.2	
Total		40.1	

Exhibit 3-1 continued

Other Specialties

Anesthesiology	8.6
Child psychiatry	3.7
Emergency medicine	5.6
Neurology	2.3
Nuclear medicine	1.6
Pathology	5.6
Preventive medicine	3.0
Psychiatry	15.8
Radiology	7.4
All other and unspecified	6.7
Total	60.3
Total Physicians	191.4

3. Your hospital's medical staff analysis:

		M.D.'s	D.O.'s
a.	Number of physicians on active staff:	_____	_____
b.	Number of physicians on courtesy staff:	_____	_____
c.	Number of physicians on dental staff:	_____	_____
d.	Number of physicians on consulting staff:	_____	_____
e.	Number of physicians admitting 80% of patients:	_____	_____

   Names: _____

   _____

   _____

   f. Number of physicians admitting *one* patient
      last month: _____   _____

   g. Age of physicians: _____ _____ _____
                         25–40   41–64   65+

   h. Does the hospital have residents or interns? _____
      From what school? _____

   i. Office buildings:
      Where is the nearest doctor's office building?

      _____

      _____

   j. Does the hospital own or lease any buildings? _____
      What is the occupancy? _____

   k. Is there a need for additional space? _____

   l. Medical staff officers   Specialty
      President _____   _____
      Vice president _____   _____
      Secretary _____   _____
      Past president _____   _____
      Medical director _____   _____
      Term of office _____   _____

   m. Significant problems/needs _____

      _____

      _____

Exhibit 3-1 continued

4. Nursing analysis (shortage versus supply): _____

_____

_____

_____

E. *Administration*
   1. Main concerns of administrator: _____

_____

_____

_____

_____

   2. Main concerns of governing board: _____

_____

_____

_____

_____

   3. Other comments: _____

_____

_____

_____

_____

*Source of 1990 data is U.S., Department of Health and Human Services, *Graduate Medical Education National Advisory Committee (GMENAC) Summary Report* (Washington, D.C.: U.S. Government Printing Office, 1980). *Source:* Leora Udkoff, *Sample Market Analysis* (Encino, Calif.: Hyatt Medical Enterprises, 1981.)

NOTES

1. David D. Karr, "Increasing Hospital's Market Share," *Journal of American Hospital Association,* June 1, 1977, p. 64.

2. *Public Law, 95-142,* 91 Stat 1175, Oct. 25, 1977.

3. "Washington Briefs," *Modern Health Care,* December 1979, p. 24.

4. Robin E. MacStavic, *Marketing Health Care* (Rockville, Md.: Aspen Systems Corp., 1977), pp. 52–63.

5. Ibid., pp. 88–97.

6. Philip Kotler, *Marketing for Non-Profit Organizations* (Englewood Cliffs, N.J.: Prentice-Hall, 1975), p. 125.

Chapter 4

Recruitment Program Options

Physician recruitment should be considered a part of a hospital's master plan and as a necessary and integral function of the hospital's operations. In the best of all possible worlds, a hospital administrator would be able to devote a major portion of time to physician recruitment. This unfortunately is not always possible because of the complexities of a hospital's day-to-day operations. Nevertheless, physician recruitment should still be a part of daily operations and, in fact, should be implemented on an ongoing basis.

As we have seen in previous chapters on need determination and marketing, the best time to implement a recruitment program is when the need has not yet reached a desperate or crisis level. The hospital administration should be alerted to an impending physician shortage crisis if a heavy admitter decides, without any notice, to leave the community for personal reasons; if a group of doctors that represent 80 percent of the hospital's admissions breaks up because of interpersonal problems and several leave the community altogether; if a director of a medical department decides to leave at a moment's notice; or if 75 percent of the medical staff is 50 years of age or older and no new physicians have entered the community in the last three years. All of these are examples of events that can trigger a physician shortage crisis. If a program is developed in stages prior to such potential crises, however, there is a greater chance of it being successful on an ongoing basis.

SELECTION CRITERIA

Before initiating a physician recruitment program, a decision must be made by the planning committee as to which type of program will be in the best interest of the hospital and the community it serves. This decision will determine the role of the recruitment committee in the recruitment process. There are basically four program options available to the planning committee, each differing with respect to the degree of involvement that the committee undertakes in relation to an outside consulting firm in the planning and/or implementation stages:

1. The facility may develop and implement its physician recruiting program completely on its own.
2. It may subcontract the planning and development stages to an outside recruiting firm but implement the program itself.
3. It may do the planning and development of the program itself but subcontract the implementation stages.
4. It can subcontract with an outside recruitment firm to undertake the entire recruiting program.

In order to decide which type of recruitment program to adopt, six basic criteria should be evaluated with relation to the particular hospital and its physician need:[1]

1. level of expertise
2. time investment
3. available funds
4. retention rate
5. impact on the existing health care system
6. success of program on an ongoing basis

After reviewing the guidelines and the criteria involved in each type of program, as detailed in the following paragraphs, a decision can be made as to which alternative will best meet the needs of the hospital and its community.

Level of Expertise

The field of hospital administration has grown to such an extent over the past few years that it has become increasingly difficult for one person to command all the skills necessary to operate a hospital. The position of hospital administrator demands both technical and administrative skills and also a tremendous amount of time investment. Before an administrator can decide if the hospital should undertake a physician recruitment program completely on its own, the following questions should be considered:

• What is the administrator's actual experience in developing a recruitment program?
• How successful has that experience been in the past?

- What is the administrator's knowledge of the field?
- If the experience is lacking, can this kind of expertise be found from other sources?

Often a hospital administrator will not have the comprehensive knowledge of how to set up a recruitment program. Unaware of the problems of using only one source for input, the administrator may rely entirely on the hospital's medical staff. There is no question that a hospital's medical staff can provide necessary and valuable input; however, it should not be the only source. When evaluating the resources available to augment recruiting experience and expertise, one should make sure that there is a mixture of information sources available for use. Such a mix will provide the administrator with a more unbiased approach in recruiting physicians to the facility.

Time Investment

A major investment of time is involved in developing and implementing a successful physician recruitment program. Considerable time is needed to make a needs determination for the hospital. This type of indepth analysis and research requires a great deal of attention before the actual recruitment efforts can begin. Once the recruitment process is underway, it involves ongoing discussions with potential physicians—not only daily, but at times even hourly. This time requirement can be sporadic or steady, entailing persistent follow-up and contact. Weak follow-up by the administrator with a potential physician recruit can jeopardize the entire recruitment process. Consistent feedback and timing are the crucial elements for program success.

Available Funds

The physician recruitment process can be a very costly project. To develop an appropriate program, it is necessary to invest dollars as well as time. Expenditures include the fees and costs of printing of informational brochures; advertisements in professional journals and other publications; long-distance telephone calls, mailings, letters, and postage; the use of placement listings; travel by the hospital administrator to other areas to make contacts; and visits to the community by prospective recruits and their families.

The costs of community visits in the physician recruitment process can be quite high. If the hospital is located on the East Coast and is bringing in a physician and spouse from the West Coast for an interview, the outlay can be substantial. Besides the costs associated with planning, development, and interviewing, the expenses involved in assisting a physician to begin a practice, such as relocation and office expenses, are additional factors that must be taken into account when embarking upon a physician recruitment program.

Another important factor affecting the cost of the program is the length of time the recruitment efforts will continue. Obviously, these efforts must continue until the necessary physicians have been recruited, but there is no exact way to predict how long it will take for the program to be successful. The use of a tentative budget is one way to monitor these costs; however, the budget will have to be flexible in order to meet all of the demands of the physician recruitment effort. In many cases, how much money a hospital can allocate to a physician recruitment program will determine whether it will seek outside assistance and to what extent.

Retention Rate

The retention rate is an important measure of how successfully the recruitment program is functioning. Will the physicians attracted in the physician recruitment program stay as members of the medical staff for a significant period of time? Is the program so well-organized that, once the physicians have relocated to the community, their needs will be satisfactorily met, ensuring their retention?

Positive involvement with members of the existing medical staff will promote the retention of a new physician recruit. With active medical staff support for the hospital's recruitment efforts, the physicians will be more supportive of the incoming physician, which will facilitate a subsequent higher physician retention rate.

Impact on the Existing Health Care System

In developing the hospital's physician recruitment program, it is important to consider what impact the program will have on the existing health care system. Conflicts can arise if the need for additional physicians does not coincide with the planning guidelines formulated by the area's health systems agency or other prevailing regulatory agencies. The recruitment of a specialty physician to a hospital may lead to the need for additional services and/or beds. If the regulatory agency does not approve the addition of such services, the needs of the recruited physician may not be fulfilled.

Regionalization can have an impact upon the hospital's physician need. For example, if perinatal regionalization is introduced to the area and the hospital is identified as a primary Level-I provider, the need for highly specialized obstetricians may not be indicated. However, this might conflict with the hospital's perceived need to recruit additional obstetricians to the facility. All such changes and trends in the health care arena should be carefully considered before implementing the physician recruitment program.

Success of Program on an Ongoing Basis

A physician recruitment program is not just a single directed effort; it is composed of many coordinated endeavors. It is thus an ongoing process and should be monitored by the hospital administrator on that basis. One way to determine the success of the program is to look at its ability to locate potential physician recruits. Another measure is whether the recruited physician stays in the community and for how long.

Evaluation of the program's success on an ongoing basis will facilitate the means to deal with target problems as they occur and to provide timely solutions. This evaluation will also assist the hospital in determining to what extent it may need the services of an outside firm.

PROGRAM OPTIONS

An analysis of the above discussed selection criteria will help the hospital select that program option—developing and implementing its own program; developing its own program and subcontracting for implementation; subcontracting the planning stages and implementing its own program; or subcontracting for both the planning and the implementation stages—that best meets the requirements of the planning committee.

The Hospital Develops and Implements Its Own Program

The first program option is the development and implementation of the hospital's own physician recruitment efforts. In order for a hospital to undertake a program on its own, it is necessary to have access to extensive experience, money, and time. Both functions of the program—the planning and its implementation—will be the administrator's responsibility. Indeed, with only one person coordinating both functions, a smoother transition between steps can be anticipated.

Outline of a Physician Recruitment Program

The following outline of a physician recruiting program, developed by an individual administrator and then submitted to a board of directors as a starting point to solve a hospital's physician recruitment needs, highlights the hospital's physician needs, the candidate sources, the money available, and the step-by-step process of implementing the program.[2] The outline is not intended to be a detailed blueprint for developing a recruitment program; it is intended rather to serve as a general guideline to aid hospitals in recruiting physicians to their areas.

Purpose. The physician recruiting program is designed to provide an outline of how the board of directors, the administration and the medical staff can identify physician needs for the hospital and community and how these needs will be filled. The program will also serve as a guideline for the hospital administration in allocating resources and in efforts to attract and retain physician candidates who wish to locate in the community.

Physician Needs. There must be a defined process for identifying physician needs to ensure the continued success of the hospital and to meet existing and future community needs. There are several ways to determine these needs:

- A periodic survey of the medical staff. At least annually the medical staff will be polled to determine if there are physician needs to improve or expand the physician services of the community.
- An input or consideration of community needs. The board of directors, the administration, or other members of the community will be asked to present ideas concerning possible requirements to meet certain community needs.
- Hospital administration review. The administrator will review the hospital medical staff for utilization and needs at least annually, providing a report of those physician needs that will or may be required to ensure the continued success of the hospital.

In order to coordinate and unify these needs, the joint conference committee of the board and medical staff or a committee selected by the board will review the input from the above sources. After review of the input, the committee will determine the priorities of the needs that should be acted upon and who will undertake the recruiting effort.

Sources of Potential Candidates. When a physician need has been identified, a multisource approach will be used to locate potential candidates to fill the identified needs. The following sources will be used:

- physicians on staff
- contacts with local and area medical schools and programs
- advertisements in national and specialty journals
- physician recruiting firm(s)

When information on a potential candidate has been received by the hospital administrator, it will be presented for review to the joint conference committee or a committee selected by the board. When and if the committee agrees that the individuals are qualified potential candidates, the recruiting process will continue.

Resources Allocation. The recruitment of physicians will require the allocation of financial resources both for the direct recruitment of the physicians and for the retention of potential candidates.

The financial resources for direct recruitment will cover the following items:

- advertising: approximate costs, $1,200
- development of brochures and other information: approximate costs, $4,000 to $6,000
- travel and entertainment: approximate costs, $3,000 to $5,000
- relocation of new physicians: approximate costs, $5,000 to $10,000
- use of recruiting firm: approximate costs, $8,000 to $10,000 per physician

The financial resources for the retention of candidates will cover guarantees for physicians who locate in the community. The guarantees will be in the form of monies to ensure the physicians against their net collections. Suggested guarantees to be offered are, for general or family practitioners, $50,000 per year or $4,200 per month against net collections and, for specialists, $60,000 or more per year, depending on the specialty involved.

Other financial incentives could include subsidized office rent for three to six months and assistance in paying for office personnel. They may also include advances or loans to cover the first quarter of malpractice insurance or loans for equipment in the physician's office.

Recruiting Process. The success of the recruiting program will depend on the involvement of the three main segments of the hospital—the board of directors, the medical staff and the hospital administration. Thus, it will be necessary to establish a recruiting committee with board members, medical staff members, and members of the administration as representatives. This committee will oversee and direct the recruiting program.

The following general steps are involved in the recruitment of physicians. First, the need must be identified. Then, a search for candidates must be initiated. Interested candidates should be provided information about the area. Then, the candidates should be screened in a review of their curricula vitae. Thereafter, a decision should be made either to invite or not to invite the candidate for a site visit. If the decision is to invite the candidate to visit, the administrator will contact the candidate to arrange the visit.

Upon arrival for the visit, the candidate will be picked up by the administrator or another committee member. The candidate will then be shown the community and surrounding area and entertainment will be provided. The candidate should meet with several members of the committee and other practicing physicians in the community.

The administrator will follow up with the candidate regarding interest in locating in the community. Answers to the candidate's questions and other information will be provided as needed. If another site visit is necessary, it should be arranged at this time.

When a physician decides to locate in the community, coordination of efforts should begin in the following areas: (1) moving of household effects and a welcome to the community; (2) making sure that the office is ready and equipped for occupancy; (3) announcements and an open house before and upon opening of the office; (4) helping the physician to obtain housing; (5) making school arrangements for the physician's children; (6) helping the physician's spouse obtain a job, if necessary; (7) working with the bank on financing, if needed; and (8) other tasks that will make the relocation of the physician into the community as smooth and painless as possible.

Physician Recruitment from the Administrator's Perspective

The following outline provides a second viewpoint on physician recruitment.[3] Although there are many similarities to the preceding outline, one can observe that different concerns are being voiced here by an executive of a large hospital management company.

First, it is necessary to determine why the hospital needs to recruit physicians: to replace an aging medical staff? to add subspecialists? to replace critical physicians who are leaving the area? because of census problems? in response to community need? The "why" of recruitment must be determined *before* the process starts.

Second, a medical staff analysis must be completed. The key to identifying need is to analyze existing medical staff characteristics in conjunction with overall hospital need. Key areas in this analysis are the ratio of generalists to specialists, age, admissions per month, vacation patterns, pending retirements or slow-downs, and future needs in terms of hospital programs.

Third, the existing medical staff should be utilized. The existing staff and the physicians in the immediate area offer the most expedient short-term means of solving a census problem. Physicians who are geographically close to the area will know the medical facilities and other physicians and can serve as an immediate resource for short-term recruitment needs. Marketing services to these professionals may help them to change their practice patterns in favor of your facility.

Fourth, resources beyond the local area should be analyzed. In this effort, however, it is desirable to recruit candidates who are generally familiar with your area or who have an interest that is compatible with the community and its surrounding resources. An urbanized physician may not be interested in locating to a rural or semirural area. Conversely, a physician who likes to fish and hunt may be opposed to urban living.

There are a number of ways to solicit candidates for recruitment. In addition to contacts with local resources, state medical societies, and the AMA, a valuable recruiting source is a professional agency that specializes in this field. While fees of $8,000 to $10,000 may seem expensive in terms of individual candidate recruitment, the fee may be quickly offset by revenue gains at the hospital. An average physician practicing at a hospital may produce revenues in excess of $200,000 a year. As a return on investment, this ratio is very favorable.

Fifth, various methods of financing should be explored. It is not unusual, even in the larger metropolitan areas, for physicians to expect some type of financial assistance. This aspect should be addressed prior to the initiation of recruitment efforts. The provision of office space, free or subsidized, and other types of office support—for example, aid in billing, personnel, or data processing—may be considered.

Many physicians have become accustomed to a minimum guarantee, which ranges upwardly from $40,000, plus malpractice insurance. If they are capable and aggressive, physicians on a guarantee will rarely be a drain on such resources. Most young physicians will exceed their guarantee if their practices become moderately active.

In lieu of minimum guarantees, loan guarantees at low interest or at no interest are also possible considerations. The advantage of the loan guarantee is that the physician is obligated to pay back the financial support, and, as a result, the community does not feel that special gifts have been made to a privileged physician. Moreover, once a loan fund has been established, it can be reused in other recruiting efforts.

Sixth, membership or partnership in some sort of group or practice may be an important consideration. Older physicians particularly may be looking for a young associate to take over their practice load and allow them to phase out or to retire. These situations should be identified.

Seventh, the interview process should be a personalized experience. Indeed, the interview should be a very personal experience for both the physician and the physician's spouse. A well-organized agenda that is focused on selling your community, your facility, and the desirability of family life at your location is an important asset. Medical staff members should be included in the interview process.

Eighth, certain pitfalls must be avoided. Many practitioners already established at your facility may not appreciate the need to recruit new physicians to their community; afterall; they may be working hard in their practices and may not like to see potential competition. This might affect the interview process, and it certainly will affect the welcome received by a new arrival.

Finally, it should be remembered that successful recruitment occurs not only at the interview but when the physician arrives. The physician's welcome to the community, or the lack thereof, can easily affect the decision to stay. A new arrival should be assisted whenever possible. This is an administrative responsibility; but physicians who understand the need and do not feel threatened may also want to help the new arrival along. A "buddy system" with another physician for the first few weeks may be fruitful. Introductions to specialists, to other hospital-based physicians or to other friends at lunch and other such gestures will help the new physician adjust and meet more quickly the needs of your facility. All these considerations are important in establishing a practice and referral patterns for the new arrival.

Types of Assistance Extended to Physician Recruits

Following are specific areas in which assistance may be provided to a physician recruit or a newly arrived physician.

The Realtor. Showing the residential living characteristics of your community is a key part of the recruitment process. Time should be spent with a *quality* realtor who is interested in selling the community first, and a house second. Inappropriate, negative discussions about the area may serve to terminate the interview process. Discussions about forced busing, crime problems, and inappropriate ethnic opinions are all potential "turnoffs" that may offend the candidate.

Banks. A physician may be the world's worst businessman, but that is not the way most physician's perceive themselves. A physician will want to be a "preferred customer" at the local bank and will also want to have a professional contact with someone with enough authority to contribute to key decisions. A credit line greater than that which an average person requires may be desirable. Most branch managers of large banks have rather low loan authority limits and, therefore, may not be the best contacts. On the other hand, many larger banks have special staffs that deal specifically with professional clientele. In any case, it is appropriate to seek out key banking executives to help in the recruitment process.

Certified Public Accountants. The establishment of a practice and the use of financial planning methodology involve more effort and specialized knowledge and training than ever before. An introduction to a capable CPA and/or a certified financial planner may thus serve as a very positive incentive for the physician. Assisting the physician to establish a practice from a business perspective can be a substantial benefit in the recruitment process.

Insurance. Those professional individuals who can assist the physician in acquiring appropriate insurance of all types should be identified in advance. They should be individuals with a long-range prospective rather than a short-range commission attitude. Malpractice, liability, homeowners, and automobile insurance policies are all part of a comprehensive insurance package.

Interior Decorator. A well-qualified interior designer may be needed to assist new physicians in establishing their offices or homes. Such an individual can be very helpful to both the physician and the physician's spouse.

Of course, all of the above-mentioned people should have been contacted prior to the physician's arrival, should understand the interview process, and be willing to help sell the opportunity. The business will follow, if, and only if, the physician is interested in coming to the community.

Specialized Material. Information about the hospital, its competition, and its growth plans and future are integral to the interview. The characteristics of the medical staff and community practitioners are fundamental from the physician's point of view. Such information should be tailored specifically to each new physician. The more information that can be provided concerning the new environment the better basis the physician will have for making a positive decision. In this connection, a medical staff application, the hospital bylaws, chamber of commerce information, the hospital annual report, and other pertinent information such as a master plan should be included to help the interviewee make an intelligent decision. Most physicians will be keenly interested in the hospital and its future in making their practice decision.

Summary

The two perspectives on physician recruitment outlined above are quite different, yet both cover basically the same information. In order to establish a physician recruitment program independently, it is necessary to be aware of all of the elements mentioned. The main consideration, however, is to organize the program prior to its implementation.

In short, the recruitment process is much more complex than might have been anticipated. A well-planned recruitment methodology, with strong assistance at all points, will improve the success rate. It will indicate to the physician that you are well-organized and sincere in your recruitment efforts.

Finally, to reiterate, the spouse of the physician is an important part of the recruitment process and should be considered during the *entire* interview.

The Hospital Develops Its Own Program and Subcontracts Out the Implementation

Most hospital administrators have a good sense of the pulse of their medical communities. Because the administrator is familiar with the nature and habits of the medical staff, the hospital, and the surrounding community, it might be easier for the hospital to develop its own recruitment program. If it decides to do so, however, it should be aware that a great deal of time and expertise will be required.

At the developmental stage, the funds expended are minimal compared to the time invested. Thus, more money can be allocated to the implementation stage, which can be executed by an external firm. At the same time, so much groundwork will have been done by the administrator and staff that the time expenditure will not be as great during the implementation stage.

If the hospital develops its own need analysis and the initial stages of the recruitment program, it is likely to achieve a greater retention rate. Many more hospital people will be involved in the beginning stages, working toward not only attracting but also retaining the physician.

The Hospital Subcontracts the Planning Stages but Implements Its Own Program

Many administrators feel that the most expedient way to analyze their medical communities is to subcontract with an outside firm to identify present medical staff patterns and to develop a plan for future trends. This frees the administrator from this task, but permits a review and analysis of the material after it is compiled. Many administrators who have utilized this method have been very pleased with the results.

For the most part, the firms that are utilized are marketing companies that are concerned with the developmental stages of the recruitment program. It is very important for the administrator, however, to be concerned as well with the following implementation phase. Although there are differing views regarding planning and implementation in the field of physician recruitment, it is clear that the two functions must be interrelated. If a decision is made to subcontract the planning stages of the program, it is important to discuss with the outside firm the hospital's capabilities and limitations for implementing the recruitment plan.

In working with an outside firm, it is imperative to (1) develop a weekly reporting system so that the outside firm can report on a timely basis and the administration can monitor the direction of the proposed plan, (2) develop an outline of the firm's activities that defines areas of responsibility during a designated time period, (3) set up at the outset a timetable for various aspects of the plan, and (4) allocate funds for the first phase of the recruitment process.

It is very important to determine in advance the cost of the final product. When subcontracting the planning stages for program development and receiving the consultant's recommendations, the administration should remember that it will be the hospital's ultimate responsibility to implement the recruitment plan.

In summary, when an outside consulting firm is used, it is important to set guidelines in advance, to stay involved in a supervisory capacity so that monitoring can occur, and to review the results of the developmental plan with an eye toward its implementation.

The Hospital Subcontracts Out Both Planning and Implementation Stages

If a hospital chooses to subcontract out the entire physician recruitment program, it should understand that there is a definite risk in not being actively involved in the process. In this case, it should be very sure that the subcontracted firm is able to plan as well as implement the program within a specified budget during a specified period of time. The program must provide the required retention rate and at the same time not have a negative effect on the existing medical community.

In general, we would not recommend that a hospital subcontract for an entire recruitment program. It is very important that the hospital administration stay involved in all levels of planning, development, and implementation. The input of the hospital administrator is critical, with the degree of involvement dependent upon the administrator's available time and capabilities.

SUMMARY

The first three program options we have discussed provide the administration and the board of trustees with certain levels of involvement. It is possible to blend several of these options to accommodate the administrator's level of expertise and the time the administrator and staff are willing to commit. If the administrator decides to delegate the entire project to an external firm, the hospital is definitely taking a risk. It must be very confident that the selected firm can perform.

After the hospital has performed the physician need and market analysis and feels comfortable in the selection of one of the program options, it must determine the criteria for selecting an outside firm, if one is to be used, to assist it in its physician recruitment program.

The criteria for determining which firm is best suited for a particular hospital are the same as those used in selecting the program option. The major considerations are the firm's level of expertise, the time that will be spent in working with it, the money that will be spent for the firm's services, the method selected to assist the hospital to retain recruited physicians, and the impact the firm will have on the medical community.

NOTES

1. Suzanne McNeely Lewitt, "How To Judge the Value of What You Spend on Physician Recruitment" (Paper presented at Association of California District Hospitals, Lake Tahoe, May 1980), pp. 2–8.

2. Material in this section was adapted from Thomas Fite, "Physician Recruiting Program" (Canoga Park, Calif.: Author, © 1978), pp. 1–6. Used by permission.

3. Material in this and the following sections was adapted from Ryland P. Davis, "Physician Recruitment from the Administrator's Perspective" (Dublin, Calif.: Author, © 1979), pp. 1–9. Used by permission.

Chapter 5

Recruitment Firms

When health care executives do not have the time to develop and implement their own physician recruitment program, it will be necessary, as we have noted, to select an outside firm to assist at various levels of development or implementation. Before making the selection, the planning committee must decide which firm is best suited for its particular situation. Consulting firms, like hospitals, have unique characteristics that distinguish them. The selection criteria should enable the planning committee to evaluate each physician recruitment firm on its merits and ultimately to select that company that is most compatible with the hospital's needs.

TYPES OF RECRUITMENT FIRMS

The numerous recruitment firms throughout the country can be distinguished by the types of services they render, by the compensation and method of payment to the firm, and by the remuneration system for the firm's employees. Given these distinguishing characteristics, there are basically three forms of companies that provide recruitment services: (1) placement agencies; (2) search consultant firms; and (3) byproduct firms, including marketing-consulting firms.

Placement Agencies

Placement agencies are perhaps the best known of the three kinds of recruitment firms. Placement agencies, also known as executive search firms, have been in existence for many years. Such agencies provide a very valuable service, freeing the administrator and hospital staff from performing exhaustive searches that may or may not result in attracting qualified candidates. A reputable agency will identify and screen the candidates, enabling the hospital to make a selection based on several interested applicants.

Whenever a hospital is in need of executive personnel, administrators should consider the option of utilizing a placement agency. In terms of physician recruitment, however, which is a specialized field, there can be some drawbacks that a hospital should be aware of before employing the services of a placement agency. Such an agency must place large numbers of people in order to remain financially solvent, because a large portion of the finder's fee is paid to the agency employee in the form of a commission. Therefore, it is necessary for the agency to keep overhead to a minimum, while at the same time attracting many clients. Because telephone contacts involve a lot less overhead than personal contacts they are the primary method this type of agency uses to attract physicians. Still, if the hospital is willing to do a great deal of the prescreening, administrators may wish to utilize a placement agency to obtain a large number of curricula vitae, which they in turn can review and use for making contacts.

Placement agencies are paid by the client on a contingency basis which is based on successful performance. This structure requires that agencies work with large numbers of clients, which could decrease the personalized attention a physician recruitment program requires.

Usually, a placement agency recruits more than just physicians. If the individual recruiter is dependent on the commission structure for earning a living, immediate placements are sought. Immediate placement is certainly a plus factor for the hospital; but, in terms of physicians, it may not be possible. This is due to the fact that the majority of physicians available for recruitment are graduating residents. These physicians are usually completing their training and are not available for relocation for a period of six months to perhaps a year. This time lag may result in the hospital not receiving sufficient attention from the placement agency to complete a long-range physician recruitment program.

Search Consultant Firms

A search consultant firm provides a tailored service adapted to the specific needs of the client and embodying the marketing skills that are so vital to the physician recruitment effort. In attempting to attract a physician to the community, a search consultant works toward becoming an extension of hospital administration. This necessitates an indepth analysis of community needs, existing medical staff concerns, and present referral patterns. A good search firm will attempt to match these elements with physicians who are qualified, interested in the area, and serious about relocation. A search firm will identify these physicians, be actively involved in the interview, area visit, and follow-up, and will do everything possible to assist the client in recruiting the physician.

The search firm will contact available physicians through a comprehensive network involving personal contacts, residency program presentations, visits to national conventions, referrals from other physicians, and seminars and other environments that allow the search consultant to meet available physicians and evaluate their qualifications before introducing the physician to the client.

The fee for the services of a search firm is usually a combination of a nonrefundable retainer and an additional fee due after successful relocation of the physician. Search firm recruiters are normally paid a salary plus a bonus based on performance. By becoming an extension of the hospital, a search consulting firm adds another dimension to the existing recruitment efforts of the facility.

Byproduct Firms

A byproduct firm is a company that provides secondary services for a separate fee as a byproduct of its main business. This is common with many marketing companies, consulting firms, and emergency room groups. For example, a marketing firm performs a needed service and can free the administrator from many unnecessary tasks, allowing more freedom in decision making. The impact of basic marketing skills and techniques applied in the preparation of a physician recruitment program is obvious. When the marketing company is hired to do an indepth analysis of an existing medical community, it becomes very knowledgeable about the situation and can generally implement the recommended program suggested. If, however, the company's initial involvement with the hospital was merely to generate a report without providing any additional services, an additional fee will normally be due when successful physician recruitment occurs.

Emergency room groups will often obtain emergency room contracts based on the fact that they have assisted the local community in recruiting physicians. In one case, an emergency room contract was awarded to a large physician group because it guaranteed the hospital that, through its membership, it would find a specialist needed in the community. In this case, there was no additional fee because the contract awarded to them provided enough remuneration.

Consulting and marketing groups usually charge a fee, called a "finder's fee," normally based on performance. Like search consulting firms, however, byproduct firms usually pay their employees salaries as remuneration. If the employees are active and successful in recruiting, they will normally receive a bonus or a percentage for each placement they make.

ASSESSMENT CRITERIA

It is very difficult in the health care field to evaluate and assess the many recruitment companies available. The following assessment criteria will help in judging which type of firm will best meet the needs of the hospital and community.[1]

Experience

Previous experience in the health care field is of crucial importance when assessing a recruitment agency's qualifications. Experience in executive search does not necessarily ensure success in the area of physician recruitment. There are very few companies that do only physician recruitment. When reviewing and evaluating a placement agency, the hospital must be very sure that the agency has had successful experience in physician recruitment, not merely executive search.

Scope of Knowledge

Another important factor to be considered is whether the firm has a working knowledge of the health care field as it relates to physician recruitment. The firm must be able to answer the following questions:

- What are the laws in the state that affect physician recruitment? This is a very important question because these laws can shape efforts in establishing an initial physician recruitment program.
- What type of federal legislation can affect recruitment? It is very important that the agency is aware of these laws so that they can assist the hospital to stay within the federal guidelines.
- What are the physician licensing laws and malpractice regulations for the state? It is an expensive mistake to recruit physicians who cannot ultimately be licensed in a particular state. Different licensing requirements relate to foreign medical graduates and osteopathic physicians.

Not all states have the same standards or requirements. It is therefore very important that the recruitment agency knows the licensing laws for the area and is able to assist in contacting the appropriate people if there are questions to be answered. This also applies to the malpractice regulations in the state. The agency should be knowledgeable of the various malpractice regulations, insurance policy underwriters, differences between claims made and occurrence coverage, insurance rates in the area, and extent of the coverage.

An important factor to consider is whether the planning activities of the health systems agency, or other prevailing regulatory agencies in effect at the time, will affect physician recruitment. Will there be drastic changes in the health delivery system in the near future that might indicate the need for a certain specialty that is not indicated at the present time? The hospital should be aware of these local changes and make sure that the agency selected is able to work within the guidelines.

Another important factor is an understanding of the medical community. Does the firm have a relationship with the existing medical community? Is it aware of the significance of the present referral patterns? Is it aware of the relationship of the hospital to the physicians in the service area? Is it acquainted with the feelings of the present medical community, particularly as they relate to new physicians? To ensure successful recruitment, it is very important that the existing medical community be understood and involved with the recruitment program at all stages.

Method of Recruitment

What is the method the firm utilizes in recruiting physicians? Is it strictly on a referral basis, utilizing the mail and phone, or is there indepth prescreening of the physician? Does the firm perform on-site visits? Will the administrator have an opportunity to meet with the recruiters? Do the recruiters assist in follow-up activities? These are all extremely important activities that a firm should perform in order to be successful in recruiting physicians.

Specifically, a competent firm should perform the following:

• assist the hospital in organizing community support
• interview as many physicians as possible within the medical community and provide feedback to the recruitment committee
• assist in defining areas of responsibility so that when a physician visits the community the interview will run smoothly

In many cases, the success or failure of recruitment efforts will depend on how well the interview was perceived by the visiting physician and spouse. A recruitment firm should assist in developing this program and in helping with the implementation stages.

Stability Track Record

How long has the firm been in business? Does the firm provide a list of references? Are these references board members as well as administrators? Can the firm provide the names of physicians that it has successfully relocated? Since physician retention is such an important aspect of the planning program, the stability and the track record of the company are of primary concern.

Fee/Payment Schedule

Various types of agencies charge different fees and have different payment schedules. Most placement agencies charge on a contingency basis (after placement occurs). This fee is based normally on the percentage of the physician's estimated compensation in the first year. This percentage is usually 15 to 25 percent of the physician's first year's gross income, although in some areas the fees are as high as 35 percent.

If there is no guarantee of salary involved, it is difficult to determine the estimated gross income. In this case, a flat fee is normally charged. This fee can be as little as $6,000 or as much as $15,000. However, the method of charging a percentage of a physician's first-year income is not always compatible with the goals of a physician recruitment program.

Search firms normally require a nonrefundable retainer that initiates the search process. The firm then collects an additional fee when successful relocation occurs. This retainer is approximately 25 to 50 percent of the total fee. The total fee is based on an estimate of the effort and time necessary to complete the search. A typical search fee is $8,000 to $12,000 per recruited physician.

The method of payment for a placement agency is also different from that of a search firm. A placement agency usually divides the payment into two or three equal installments. If there are three installments, the first is normally due when the physician signs the contract, the second is due when the physician initiates practice, and the final installment is due at some later date following a guarantee period. If there are two installments, the first is normally due when the physician initiates the practice, and the second is due at the end of the guarantee period.

A search firm charges a nonrefundable retainer that is paid when the contract is signed. The remaining portion is paid when the physician is successfully recruited. In most cases, half of the remaining fee is paid when the physician begins his practice, and the other half is due at a certain time in the future, based on the guarantee period. It is necessary to determine the payment schedule in advance and to make arrangements so that cash flow will not be a problem when the payments are due.

Follow-Up Activities

Another criterion for judging agencies is the extent of follow-up activities performed. Does the firm assist in practice management advice? A physician who is beginning practice needs assistance regarding office space, space planning, equipment, billing procedures, and office help—in short, in all of the many related business functions that are a part of establishing a practice.

Does the agency assist in any way during this period? Does it give advice? Does it refer the physician to other individuals who provide these services? Does it provide any information on the leasing and buying of equipment? Does it provide advice on office rental? In other words, is it knowledgeable in areas that directly affect the success or failure of the office practice? If a salary is being offered to the physician, does the agency offer advice regarding fringe benefits, payment of malpractice insurance, liability insurance, health insurance, workmen's compensation? Is it truly concerned with the ongoing success of the physicians, or is it simply concerned with the physician staying through the guarantee period?

THE WORKING RELATIONSHIP BETWEEN THE FIRM AND THE HOSPITAL

Working with a recruitment firm introduces temporary personnel who assist for a specified period of time in attracting physicians to the existing medical staff. Because this relationship involves dealing with new personalities, it is very important that the hospital provide a noncompetitive environment for the recruiters, both with the medical staff and in the hospital administration.

Not uncommonly, the medical staff may be very negative about assisting a recruitment firm. This can cause a lot of conflict, since the firm must work directly with the medical staff. The administration should reconsider the lines of communication if the agency is not getting full support from the medical staff members who are expected to perform follow-up activities.

Many search agreements contain exclusivity clauses to minimize conflict when a firm is working with a hospital that is also actively attempting to recruit. Because there are fees involved, it is not uncommon for a hospital to become competitive with the very firm hired to recruit. The hospital might attempt to reach a physician before a firm contacts the same physician. This can lead to an unhealthy working relationship and is not in the best interests of either the firm or the administration.

Many times a client will have unrealistic expectations about the time involved and the things that must be done to recruit physicians. Generally, it takes a minimum of one year to recruit physicians successfully. The hospital and medical board members must realize that, in order to develop a program that will guarantee continuing success, much energy must be expended and the results will not be seen overnight.

Changes in specialty requirements will also slow down the recruitment process. If this happens, an additional allowance of time should be given to the recruitment firm. If the recruitment firm is initially looking for an internist and, several months into the contract, the hospital decides that instead they really need an orthopedic surgeon, it must be understood that the firm will be starting the recruitment process over again. It is totally unrealistic to expect the original date to be fulfilled if the requirements have been changed.

Many times, misunderstandings of specific contractual relationships will stem from the initial negotiations. It is one thing to discuss the relationship prior to signing the contract; it is another to be functioning on a daily basis and find that specific elements of the initial contract are not being followed. This is why the contract should be reviewed carefully prior to implementing the program. During this review period, the various subtleties of working together should be discussed and decided. Support from both medical staff and administration is necessary at this time. The unavailability of the administration or medical staff for the interviewing process will result in a negative impression on the visiting physician and his family.

When a physician recruitment program is started, there is usually a very high level of energy, with everyone enthusiastic and wishing to participate. As the program proceeds, this enthusiasm can wane, and the follow-up, which is so crucial to success, is not done. If a firm is providing qualified, screened candidates, they may want to talk with representatives of the recruitment committee prior to scheduling an area visit. It is necessary for a committee representative to be available to speak with these physicians.

When a firm is hired, the recruitment committee may want to divorce itself from involvement, since it is the firm's responsibility to recruit the physician. This should not be allowed to happen, since it is crucial for the committee members to be available during the prescreening stage. In this way, the physicians and their families will not be making needless trips and wasting their time and that of the community members who are involved in the recruitment program. In short, it is very important that the committee members follow up promptly by speaking with candidates who have expressed a genuine interest and who have met the criteria established by the committee prior to the interviewing stage.

Nonperformance on the part of the firm should be dealt with immediately. If a firm is not performing up to the expectations of administration, special reports should be requested from the agency documenting activity. These reports should then be requested from the firm on a regular and continuing basis so that the hospital is aware of what the firm is doing on the hospital's behalf. If the firm is simply not performing at all, a meeting should be held with key personnel to determine corrective action.

In summary, based on the assessment criteria of experience, scope of knowledge, method of recruitment, stability track record, fee/payment schedule, and follow-up activities, a profile of a firm can emerge that will most closely correspond to the hospital's individual characteristics and needs.

NOTE

1. Material in this section was adapted from Suzanne McNeely Lewitt, "How To Assess Professional Recruitment Agencies and Work Effectively With Them" (Paper presented at American Hospital Association Meeting, Anaheim, Calif., September 1978), pp. 1–6.

Chapter 6

Financial Aspects

After the planning committee has reviewed the nonfinancial elements involved in recruiting physicians, and before initiating the recruitment process, it must consider the financial factors and translate them into a budget. The planning committee must educate the governing board members about the financial aspects of physician recruitment, since the board members will make the final decision involving expenditures. It is vital for the planning committee to have an allocated source of funds and an approved budget, otherwise the recruiting program will be unsuccessful and should not be undertaken.

The intent of the financial program is to concentrate on maximizing the use of funds while minimizing the expenditures. The expenditure of funds to recruit physicians impacts on the hospital, the community, and the physician in various ways. The impact on the hospital is direct and indirect. The direct impact can be seen in increased revenues. This effect is shown by the following statistics for 1979, reported by the National Center of Health Statistics:[1]

- The average physician keeps three hospital beds filled 84 percent of the time.
- Each physician's patients are hospitalized an average of 922.5 days each year.
- At $175 per patient day, hospitals receive an average of $161,000 in patient income from each physician in the United States each year.
- The average physician generates an additional $34,000 in ancillary service income.

On the average, a hospital receives approximately $200,000 in yearly income from each physician. This will vary, depending on the area of the country and the length of stay. Computations can be made for each hospital by substituting its own particular statistics.

The indirect impact on the hospital stems from the fact that better revenues allow the hospital to offer better services, which in turn may attract more physicians to the community. Increased utilization of the hospital, both on a primary and referring basis, will contribute toward making the hospital a more viable institution and fulfilling its purpose. Increased utilization will also assist in obtaining required approvals for expansion and long-term financing.

An example of this can be seen in North Carolina, where, in 1973, the Glenn R. Frye Memorial Hospital began a long-range physician recruitment program. During the period from 1975 to 1981, this hospital recruited 18 physicians, increased its services to the community by the addition of 15 new departments, and increased its bed capacity from 119 to 220.[2]

It is important to realize that, when a physician moves into a community, he has an impact on all areas of that community. He becomes a consumer as well as a spender of goods. He not only purchases capital goods—such as a home, automobile, and furnishings—but he and his wife spend money daily with local merchants. The money earned by the physician is not only spent in the community, but any excess will usually be saved in a local banking institution. The physician's practice also creates employment for nurses, technicians, and clerical staff. Finally, in addition to contributing economic benefits to the community, new physicians fulfill a need by providing services previously not available. When considering these substantial financial impacts that recruited physicians have on a community, the offer of financial assistance to a physician makes good business sense.

FINANCIAL ASSISTANCE

Many health care professionals pride themselves on their ability to recruit physicians without having to offer financial assistance. For the most part, however, an administrator will include a financial assistance package as part of a comprehensive recruiting program. In the past, such assistance was common in rural communities; but, because of increased competition, it is now also commonplace in metropolitan areas.

Often, board members who are also staff physicians will argue against financially assisting new physicians because they themselves received no assistance when starting up in the community. This can be countered with the fact that the viability of the hospital may be dependent upon the recruitment of new physicians and that to recruit these new physicians a financial incentive will be necessary. As indicated in one journal article, "it costs so much to set up a practice nowadays, that young doctors have to be commercially oriented."[3]

It is thus obvious that changed circumstances in the last decade make some kind of financial assistance necessary for the young physician who is entering private practice. This is especially true when one considers the desirable alternative choices of emergency room medicine and health maintenance organizations. These types of practice opportunities require no front-end investment; provide immediate financial rewards to the physician in the form of high salaries, limited hours, and increased benefits; but will not necessarily assist a hospital in building patient referrals.

Financial Incentive Programs

Once the planning committee recognizes the need for financial assistance, a financial incentive program should be prepared. This program should be tailored to the particular situation.

In discussing finances with a physician, it is common to encounter concerns about entering private practice due to financial requirements involving office rent, office assistance, equipment, office furniture, professional dues, malpractice insurance, medical supplies, office overhead, telephones, and so on. In addition, there are concerns about personal living expenses and the repayment of existing student and residency loans. The list of financial concerns is formidable, requiring the development of a financial incentive program that will provide the greatest benefit to the hospital with the least amount of financial exposure, while still meeting the financial needs of the physician. The three items the hospital should be most concerned with are office rental, office help, and a guaranteed income.

Office Rental

The amount of money needed for office rental depends largely on whether the physician sets up an individual office or joins an existing practice where there may be no office rent to pay. As a rule, a general practitioner needs between 800 to 1,000 square feet of space. If the hospital has available the required footage, it must be so situated within the hospital as to permit the physician's patients easy access. In this case, the only cost would be to remodel the space at a cost of about $10 to $12 per square foot, depending of course on the desired final product. The other cost to the hospital stems from the lack of reimbursement by third party payers who reimburse the hospital on a cost basis as in Medicare and Medicaid for occupancy expenses related to the portion used as medical office space.

In the event the hospital owns an office building, the remodeling costs will vary, again depending on the condition of the space to be occupied. If, for example, the space was previously occupied by a general practitioner and another one is recruited, only freshening up, in the form of flooring and wall covering, would be required. No additional office rental expenses will be incurred by the hospital because the fixed cost for mortgage payments, taxes, and general upkeep have already been incurred. In fact, in this case, after the expiration of the free office rental period, the hospital will be receiving income in the form of rent from the physician. The projected rental income will depend on the negotiation with the physician and the going rate in the community.

If the hospital does not own its own office building but wishes to provide office rental, it must seek out suitable space in a medical building, a store front with appropriate traffic patterns, or in a nonmedical professional building. The rental amount will be negotiated by the hospital but will depend on the terms that the recruited physician has agreed to, such as length of lease, escalation-of-rent clause, pass-through of expense increases from landlord to tenant, and so on. In this case, the hospital must budget an amount equal to the cost of remodeling, say, 800 to 1,000 feet, times the going rate in the community, which may vary from $.80 to $1.75 a square foot.

Lack of existing office space should not deter a hospital from entering into a recruiting program. A hospital should be creative and be able to generate office space. Obviously, the least expensive way is to have space available in the hospital or to own a building. If this is not possible, a good solution is to lease attractive trailers to house one or more physicians. Several occupied trailers can provide a strong impetus to construct a medical building, providing the nucleus for the future building's occupancy.

Office Help

When a physician enters practice, he usually is not familiar with the mechanics of opening an office. He is not knowledgeable of such things as phone answering methods, ways of scheduling appointments, means for collecting fees, billing and accounting systems, procedures for purchasing supplies, contracts with laboratories, chart keeping, and back-office procedures. The cost to the hospital for office help normally should be budgeted for about $800 to $1,200 per month for three months.

There are additional indirect costs that are not budgeted as part of the recruiting process. These costs, already incurred by the hospital, involve the time required by various hospital personnel to assist in hiring and training the office personnel. One alternative is for the hospital to pay an outside firm $4,000 to $5,000 to provide trained personnel and systems with monitoring for an additional three months. A local CPA firm may provide the service.

Guaranteed Income

A guaranteed income should be funded through a financial incentive program in one or more of the following forms:

• funds advanced by the hospital to the physician
• the hospital acting as cosigner for a loan made by a bank to the physician
• a guarantee against monthly billings made by the physician
• a guarantee against monthly collections made by the physician

A guarantee, as in the last two items above, involves a monthly payment of a variable sum determined by subtracting either the monthly billings or monthly collections, whichever is applicable, from a fixed, predetermined amount for a period of time. The period of time can be expressed either in months or until the physician reaches a certain level of billing or collections.

The guarantee on its face creates a dollar exposure equal to the fixed monthly amount less zero billings or collections. As a practical matter, and based on a great deal of experience, the actual funds advanced to the recruited physician average about $10,000 usually disbursed over a period of not less than three months and not more than six months. In some instances, especially in rural areas where there is an acute need for additional physicians, the physicians do not require advances after their first month in practice. The amount to be advanced and the period involved is in direct proportion to the degree of physician need in the community and the recruited physician's ability to build a practice. In the case of a specialist (a nongeneral practitioner), the period may be longer to allow for the establishment of referral patterns.

Billings are defined as the amount of fees for all services rendered by the physician in any one month, whether or not he actually receives payment. Collections are defined as the amount of cash actually collected by the physician for all services rendered in any one month. A physician does not have the benefit of spending his billings until collected, which is a function of time. To bridge the gap, it is customary to commit a larger guaranteed monthly amount against billings than against collections. In actuality, however, the total amounts of cash advanced are about the same in both cases.

Examples of schedules for monthly guaranteed amounts against collections and billings are shown in Tables 6-1 and 6-2 respectively.

The physician services that are rendered include not only fees generated in the office but also fees earned by working for another physician or in an emergency group. It is in the hospital's best interest to help generate income for the recruited physician without jeopardizing his opportunity to build his practice. One way of accomplishing this is to encourage the physician, if feasible, to work in the hospital emergency room (all fees so received act, in effect, as an offset to the agreed-upon advances to be made). The financial assistance agreement should provide for an uncomplicated audit procedure by the hospital to be performed prior to each monthly advance. Overfunding can result either from failing to record fees billed or collected, from recording them in the wrong month, or from a combination of both.

Funds provided by the hospital for payment of rent, office help, and guaranteed advances can be in the form of a loan to the physician to be repaid with or without interest or partial interest, in the form of a subsidy, or in some combination of a loan and subsidy. The subsidy portion does not have to be repaid.

Table 6-1 Collection Guarantee Schedule*

Month	Billing	Cash Collection	Cash Advances
1	$ 1,500	$ 500	$ 3,500
2	2,500	1,500	2,500
3	3,500	2,000	2,000
4	4,000	2,500	1,500
5	4,500	3,500	500
6	5,000	4,500	—
7	5,500	5,000	—
8	6,000	5,000	—
9	6,500	5,500	—
10	7,000	5,500	—
11	7,500	6,000	—
12	8,000	7,500	—
Total	$61,500	$49,000	$10,000

Net Result:
Total Exposure: $48,000
Actual Cash Advanced: $10,000
   *Guaranteed amount = $48,000 for 12 months or $4,000 per month against collections.
   Note: Some collection guarantees contain a provision for repayment of the advances in a sum equal to the amount collected over the total guaranteed amount ($48,000) within the guarantee period (12 months). In this example, $1,000 would be repaid in Month 13.

Table 6-2 Billing Guarantee Schedule*

Month	Billing	Cash Advances
1	$ 1,500	$3,500
2	2,500	2,500
3	3,500	1,500
4	4,000	1,000
5	4,500	500
6	5,000	—
7	5,500	—
8	6,000	—
9	6,500	—
10	7,000	—
11	7,500	—
12	8,000	—
Total	$61,500	$9,000

Net Result:
Total Exposure: $60,000
Actual Cash Advanced: $ 9,000
  *Guaranteed amount = $60,000 for 12 months or $5,000 per month against billing.

Recruitment Budget

After determining the beneficial financial impact a physician can have on a community and the usefulness of offering a financial incentive program, the next obvious concerns are: How will the funds be allocated? What additional incentives are necessary? How can the financial incentive program be translated into a recruitment budget?

A budget is only as good as the assumed variables in it, variables that change with each situation. Since the nonhospital-based physician does not generate an independent source of income for the hospital other than through the patients he admits, the budgeted items are comprised of expense items allocated for disbursement over a period of months, from the initiation of the process until the time the recruited physician is assumed to be self-sufficient.

Table 6–3 shows the basic items that should be included in the budget: the cost of brochures and printing, expenses for travel and entertainment, recruitment fees, the costs of office rental and office help, guaranteed advances, and moving expenses. Each budget a hospital prepares for physician recruiting will be different, depending on the characteristics of the particular hospital. The items in the Table 6–3 budget cover only basic expenses; the hospital may choose to exclude some of these or include additional items.

Table 6-3 Typical Budget for Recruiting a Nonhospital-Based
Physician

	During Process	Upon Relo-cation	Within 6 Mo. of Relocation	Within 1 Year of Reloca-tion	Total
Brochures, printing	$1,000	$	$	$	$ 1,000
Travel, entertainment [a]	5,000				5,000
Recruiting fees [b]	3,500	3,500	3,500		10,500
Office rental [c]			7,200	7,200	14,400
Office help [d]			3,600		3,600
Guarantee advances [e]			10,000		10,000
Moving expenses [f]		3,000			
Total	$9,500	$6,500	$24,300	$7,200	$47,500

Note: The dollar figures for this budget are based on 1981 figures and would have to be adjusted for inflation or other changes in the economy.
[a]Round trip fare paid for five physicians who visit the hospital.
[b]Assuming an agency is used.
[c]$1,200 per month, unless space is available in a medical building owned by the hospital, in the hospital, or in the office of another physician who is willing to share space.
[d]Office help for three months at $1,200 per month.
[e]Average advance based on past experience.
[f]Moving expenses, a negotiable item.

Brochures and Printing

The printing of brochures is a very important part of a successful physician recruitment program. Many of the materials that were gathered during the need and market analyses can be presented in such a way as to attract the physician and his wife. The brochures do not have to be expensive. They can be done in one color on colored stock using black-and-white photos, and they even can be typed to save the cost of typesetting. They should be purchased in a large enough quantity to provide a price break, with a ceiling of $1,000 for the final product. This cost may be greatly reduced if the local chamber of commerce already has material available. In this case, the effort should be directed toward formulating a cover letter that incorporates the data collected and addresses itself to the medical community. This cover letter can then be sent with the accompanying brochure.

Travel and Entertainment

The cost of travel will depend on the cost of transportation to the hospital from the visiting physician's point of origin. Prospective physicians' visits should be allowed with discretion so as not to result in free trips at the hospital's expense. The recruitment committee should have previously reviewed the qualifications of the physician. If an agency is used, its advice can be very valuable, since it will have had prior contact with the physician. The more attractive the area in which the hospital is located, the more visits will be requested. A visit by a serious physician without a spouse will require a second trip. Therefore, if the physician is married, the hospital should insist that his wife accompany him on the first trip. In addition to air fare, lodging, and food, an additional cost of approximately $150 per day for two people should be budgeted. In these visits, local entertainment costs will also be incurred by the hospital. Experience indicates that in order to recruit one physician, four to five physicians will visit a locale. The average cost per physician visit should not exceed $1,000.

Recruiting Fees

If a recruiting agency is part of the process, recruiting fees will be part of the basic cost. Recruiting agency fees range from a percentage of the physician's estimated income in the first year to a fixed fee payable either all in advance or as a percentage on engagement with the balance upon physician relocation. The average fee in 1981 was about $10,500 per recruited physician.

Office Rental

Office rental costs will vary depending on the location of the space. If space is available in a medical building that is owned by the hospital or is within the hospital itself, the cost will be greatly reduced. If office space is available in another physician's office and that physician is willing to share the space, the cost will also be reduced. If the hospital must provide and pay for office space, the cost allocated in the budget will depend on the going rate per square foot. Assuming the space is approximately $1 per square foot, a cost of approximately $1,200 per month for 12 months or approximately $14,400 for the year can be expected. This is a negotiable item, and, given the hospital's particular circumstances, could be greatly reduced.

Office Help

The cost of office help varies from state to state and from region to region within a state. Usually a front office receptionist will cost anywhere from $800 to $1,200 per month. Office help offered during the first few months of a physician's practice can be of great assistance to the physician during the start-up period. A hospital normally offers such office assistance for approximately three months at $1,200 per month for a total of $3,600. This, like office rent, can be negotiated if the physician would like to have the office help provided for a longer period of time with less assistance regarding office space. If office space is available through the hospital at a reduced rate, the three-month period for office help could be extended. This is a concession that the hospital may wish to consider in negotiations with the physician, setting in advance the outside parameters for this cost item.

Guaranteed Income

Guaranteed income appears to be the largest cost item in recruiting a physician. In reality, however, the actual amount of cash advanced is normally only between $4,500 and $10,000. It would be misleading to allocate the total face value of the guarantee in the budget. It would be more realistic to allocate a maximum of $10,000 for guaranteed advances (see Tables 6-1 and 6-2 for detailed information regarding this item).

Moving Expenses

Moving expenses should be considered a negotiable item in the recruiting budget; it need not be addressed until it is raised by the recruited physician. If the physician has a great deal of furniture to be moved, the issue of moving expenses may come up very early in the conversation. Because this expense is incurred at the beginning of the process, the physician will often request immediate payment. If this item is part of the financial package initially offered the physician, it might be in the best interest of the hospital to take competitive bids from several moving companies and then pay the bill directly.

Moving expenses are a budget item that has caused many hospitals to lose good physicians. Sometimes hospitals are willing to offer large amounts of money in the form of guarantees, office rent, and office help, yet they do not feel they should offer the additional $3,000 to cover moving expenses. It is not uncommon for this item to become the major issue in the negotiations. If this is the case, the hospital would be wise to consider the overall picture, to realize that the payment of moving expenses is minimal compared to the overall impact that physician will have upon the community in subsequent years.

Insurance Costs

In addition to the various miscellaneous cost factors involved in private practice that a physician may be concerned with, the cost of malpractice insurance should be considered. Depending on the specialty and the state, the cost of malpractice insurance will range from $5,000 for a general practitioner to $30,000 for an orthopedic surgeon. This amount may have to be advanced or guaranteed, but it is usually a repayable loan rather than a subsidy. If malpractice insurance is included in the budget, the repayment schedule for an appropriate period should be specified.

Equipment and Supply Costs

When setting up their offices, many physicians are concerned about payments for equipment. Funds may have to be advanced for leasing or for the down payment on equipment. Advances for these purposes should be budgeted, usually in the form of a loan with a repayment schedule stipulated. Similarly, telephone expenses and the cost of medical and office supplies may be advanced by the hospital with stipulations for repayment.

Professional Dues

Professional dues are normally paid by the physician upon entering private practice. If the physician is concerned about the payment of professional dues, however, the hospital may wish to advance funds for this purpose for the first year in the form of a loan.

Summary

In preparing a budget that includes a financial assistance program, it is important to keep the recruitment goal in mind and to consider realistically all the items to be disbursed. The goal of the facility is to attract physicians that will relocate in the community and stay for the duration of their medical career. If the hospital assists the physician in the earlier stages, using good business judgment, the physician is more likely to appreciate and support the hospital in the future.

NONHOSPITAL-BASED PHYSICIAN CONTRACTUAL ARRANGEMENTS

The areas of financial impact, financial assistance, and other budgetary concerns are prerequisite to preparing a contractual arrangement between the hospital and the recruited physician.[4] When a basic understanding between the hospital and the recruited physician has been reached regarding these issues, the understanding should be put into some form of a binding agreement. The physician will not want to incur the risks of moving without a legally enforceable contract. The hospital will desire, among other things, the physician's signature as a positive indication of his commitment to relocate.

The agreement can be in any form but should be kept as simple as possible. The physician may not have made his final decision and may be scared off by an overly imposing document. A letter of agreement, signed by the hospital and the physician, should be sufficient for this purpose.

Though simple, the agreement should clearly set forth the extent of the hospital's commitments and the basic terms and conditions of the arrangement. It is important that the hospital–physician relationship not deteriorate because the parties lacked a common understanding of the responsibilities of the physician or, more important, the benefits to be provided by the hospital.

Contract Elements

The contract should include at least the following elements:

Guarantees

The guarantee may be against the physician's billings or against actual collections. Each term should be clearly defined. For example, whether billings or collections are utilized, it is important to know whether the terms include services rendered at the hospital, compensation received from the hospital for services rendered, physician office fees, teaching or publishing fees, and so on. If collections are to be utilized, will collections received after the term of the agreement for services rendered during the term of the agreement be offset against the guarantee?

The amount of the guarantee, the method used in its calculation, and the timing for advancing the funds should be delineated. The funds could be advanced on a monthly basis, or perhaps an advance will be made prior to the commencement of the term.

The term of the agreement and/or the guarantee should be mutually agreed upon. These periods can be different. For example, funds may be advanced to the physician only over the first six months or year, but the physician may agree to remain in the community for at least two years.

Some agreements may call for repayment. For example, the hospital may agree to guarantee that the physician will receive collections of at least $60,000 in his first year in the community. The hospital may advance each month to the physician the difference between actual collections and $5,000 a month. A total of $10,000 may be advanced during the first four months, but at the end of the year the physician may have collected $70,000. The physician would then be obligated to return $10,000 to the hospital.

The agreement should set forth the procedure for repayment, the time when payments or repayments will be due, and whether a promissory note will be executed. If interest will be due on any repayment amount, that should be stipulated in the agreement. Collections received after the end of the year for services rendered during the year may trigger further repayment.

Office Space

The agreement should clearly identify the location of the office space, the period when free or reduced rent will be made available, and the extent to which the hospital or a medical building will pay for leasehold improvements. At the very least, the agreement should be clear as to the amount of the rent to be paid and the terms to which the physician is committed. The hospital should also consider having the physician execute a lease for the office space, especially to cover the period subsequent to the period of free or reduced rent.

Office Personnel

If the hospital is to provide office assistance or defray the cost of the physician's employees for a designated period, the agreement should clarify the exact terms and conditions of that relationship.

Additional Financial Incentives

The agreement should describe any other expenses to be paid by the hospital or reimbursed to the physician. For example, the hospital may pay all or a portion of the physician's moving expenses, malpractice insurance premiums, selling expenses with respect to a prior residence, or any other expenses relating either to the physician's new medical practice or the relocation process.

Commencement Date and Conditions

The agreement should require the physician to apply for medical staff privileges. If appropriate, state licensure prior to relocation and obtaining privileges and a license should be a precondition of the hospital's obligation. The agreement should include a projected date for the commencement of the guarantee and the commencement of practice in the community. Of course, if the physician cannot obtain membership on the staff, the appropriate clinical privileges, or state licensure, the agreement would not go into effect.

Enforcement

The hospital should develop a mechanism to review the physician's records in order to feel confident that the physician is acting honestly and properly under the agreement. Nothing can sour the relationship more than a feeling by the hospital that the physician is not living up to the agreement, for example, that he is obtaining cash and not reporting it.

The agreement should require the physician to work full time, to be on call at specific times, and to take a specified length of vacation. Should the physician default on the agreement, it should stipulate what, if anything, the physician must pay back to the hospital and when such payments are to be paid.

Hospital-Physician Legal Arrangements

Enforcement

Assuming (as we do) that it is legally acceptable to, at the very least, require the physician to practice in the community for a period extending beyond the period in which a guarantee is applicable, the physician can breach the agreement either before or during the guarantee period (when sums are being paid on an ongoing basis). The hospital would at that point expect repayment of the sums it advanced. These sums might not be limited to amounts payable under the guarantee, but might cover amounts actually paid or the fair market value of other inducements pursuant to the agreement. The latter exception is helpful only if an employer–employee relationship is possible under applicable state law and is determined to be bona fide.

Recently, the language regarding the extent to which the hospital can bind the physician has become substantially more general. On its face, the new language appears to be applicable to many more "business" transactions than simply kickbacks, bribes, or rebates. Language such as "any remuneration" and "directly or indirectly," has, among other things, raised justified concerns in the minds of hospital executives and attorneys throughout the nation. The concern is heightened by the fact that, while the Office of Program Integrity of the Department of Health and Human Services has the most frequent contact with the hospital associations or individual hospitals in issuing advisory interpretations of the law, the Department of Justice makes the decision as to whether to prosecute and only the courts can make a final interpretation of the law.

It is important to understand that the legality of the transaction does not depend on whether or not the hospital seeks reimbursement from the Medicare program for the costs involved in its physician recruitment programs. The critical factor is whether or not program patients are involved, not whether reimbursement is openly or covertly sought. (It has been the position of the Medicare program, supported by Provider Reimbursement Review Board decisions No. 77–D21 and 78–D27, that these costs are generally not reimbursable.[5])

Legislative Interpretations

The major recent development is the enactment of the Medicare and Medicaid Antifraud and Abuse Amendments of 1977 (Section 1877 of the

Social Security Act). Prior to these amendments, the Social Security Act, as a result of PL 92-603 (the Social Security Amendments of 1972), made kickbacks, bribes, and rebates illegal in connection with the furnishing of services covered under the Medicare or Medicaid programs. Clearly, Congress intended to make illegal "such practices as the soliciting, offering or accepting of kickbacks or bribes, including the rebating of the portion of a fee or charge for a patient referral. ... "[6]

Public Law 95-142, signed into law on October 25, 1977, substantially elaborated on this and other provisions. Section 1877 (b)(1) and (2) of this law read as follows:

> (1) Whoever knowingly and willfully solicits or receives any remuneration (including any kickback, bribe or rebate) directly or indirectly, overtly or covertly, in cash or in kind—
> (A) in return for referring an individual to a person for the furnishing or arranging for the furnishing of any item or service for which payment may be made in whole or in part under this title, or
> (B) in return for purchasing, leasing, ordering, or arranging for or recommending purchasing, leasing or ordering any good, facility, service, or item for which payment may be made in whole or in part under this title, shall be guilty of a felony and upon conviction thereof, shall be fined not more than $25,000 or imprisoned for not more than five years, or both.
> (2) Whoever knowingly and willfully offers or pays any remuneration (including any kickback, bribe, or rebate) directly or indirectly, overtly or covertly, in cash or in kind to any person to induce such person—
> (A) to refer an individual to a person for the furnishing or arranging for the furnishing of any item or service for which payment may be made in whole or in part under this title, or
> (B) to purchase, lease, order, or arrange for or recommend purchasing, leasing, or ordering any good, facility, service, or item for which payment may be made in whole or in part under this title, shall be guilty of a felony and upon conviction thereof, shall be fined not more than $25,000 or imprisoned for not more than five years, or both.[7]

Section 917 of the Medicare and Medicaid Amendments of 1980 added the words *knowingly and willfully* immediately after *whoever* at the beginning of the book, paragraphs b(1) and b(2). This can be reasonably interpreted as an indication that Congress intended to make it more difficult to violate the law through an otherwise legitimate transaction.[8]

One significant exception is found in Section 1877 (B)(3)(b), which states that the above paragraphs do not apply to "any amount paid by an employer to an employee (who has a bona fide employment relationship with such employer) for employment in the provision of covered items or services."[9] The above laws and information on the evolution of Section 1877 can be found in Volume 3 of the *CCH Medicare and Medicaid Guide.*[10]

It is of course the joint goal of the physician and the hospital that the recruitment relationship, and the contract that formalizes it, does not violate the law. Unfortunately, most laws that govern or could apply to physician-hospital relationships are very general. They do not in most cases state exactly which conduct is illegal with sufficient clarity to provide reliable guidance for those entering into this type of transaction.

Some states have laws that can be applied to physician-hospital relationships. Most of these, however, are formulated only in general terms, for example, making illegal relationships that involve kickbacks, bribes, rebates, or referral fees (usually without defining these terms). Employment of a physician by a hospital may be prohibited. However, because prosecution under these statutes is relatively rare, and because statutes are ultimately interpreted only by the courts, there are few concrete guidelines upon which to base a determination as to whether an arrangement is legal.

It is strongly recommended that the hospital's attorney be given the opportunity to review not only the substance of the arrangement between the hospital and the physician but the actual wording of the agreement as well. The binding nature of the agreement is solidified if the physician has had the agreements reviewed by an independent attorney.

Use of Hospital Facilities

The present trend appears to be that the Office of Program Integrity, in interpreting the law, is creating an exception with respect to "legitimate business transactions," as distinguished from "unethical and illegal financial arrangements (such as kickbacks, rebates or bribes)" that "unnecessarily" increase the cost of reimbursement programs.[11] Clearly, any payment that is directly or indirectly based on the volume of patients referred would be held to violate the law. Such instances would probably include:

- requiring that a physician admit his patients only to the hospital, or requiring the physician to utilize only the ancillary services of the hospital
- requiring that a specified number or percentage of the physician's patients be referred to the hospital, or basing a payment on the number or percentage of patients

- requiring that a specified number of services or specific services be rendered to the physician's hospital patients once they are admitted to the hospital, or basing a payment thereon
- requiring that a physician treat a designated number of patients (especially when there is an inherent exclusivity in the relationship between the physician and the hospital)

For example, basing the physician's discount for medical services rendered to him and his family on the number or value of services he rendered would violate the law. Essentially, any explicitly exclusive contractual referral agreement would probably violate the law. On the other hand, it appears to be acceptable to recruit a physician to a community where there is an inherent exclusive status. A hospital does not have to be a "remote or rural hospital" to be relatively sure that a physician will refer his patients to it. Even in competitive areas, if the hospital can provide convenience as well as a guarantee to the physician, it is likely that the physician will, as a practical matter, refer all or most of his patients to that hospital. At present, however, absent any explicit contractual requirement that the physician refer all (or a specific number or percentage) of his patients to a particular hospital, the general recruitment package does not appear to be treated as violative of the law.

Similarly, compensation in exchange for services not based on a level of service (such as for committee work) would appear to be acceptable. On the other hand, payments based on the number of medical records prepared would be based indirectly on the number of patients, and this could violate the law.

It does not appear to be very relevant whether the physician is being recruited away from another hospital or from another community within the same health service area. However, inducements paid to a physician who already utilizes the hospital could in many cases be more easily interpreted as based on a level of service and violative of the law.

Conclusion

It is obviously a difficult task to find the "true purpose" of a hospital's recruitment of a physician. Common sense would indicate that the hospital is making the payment with some expectation that the physician will provide a benefit to the hospital, or at least to the community. There has never been any indication from the government that such a transaction goes beyond that of a legitimate business transaction. When, and if, the government does decide that this type of transaction goes beyond a legitimate exchange, then the government may very well declare such compensation a violation of the law.

One realistic source of comfort to the hospital is that the clear language of Section 1877 (B) involves so many other normal and legitimate business transactions as to make it difficult, if not impossible, for the government to prosecute those types of arrangements that are open, aboveboard, legitimate, and in line with the guidelines cited above. For example, every time a hospital or major piece of hospital equipment is sold, a very good argument can be made that the broker, attorneys, finders, accountants, independent consultants, and business advisors (and perhaps anyone in the transaction not covered by the employee exception) are in violation of the law. Such a result was obviously not intended. Still, in all cases, the hospital, together with its legal counsel, must make an effort to determine whether or not there has been any material change in the position of the government, whether it has gone beyond the limits of a legitimate business transaction into the areas of questionable conduct indicated above.

Even though the government does not consider the costs of a recruitment program reimbursable, it has recognized their legitimacy. In one of its informal rulings related to this issue, the Office of Program Integrity has recognized that "many businesses offer financial inducements to attract competent personnel. The physician recruitment program acts to insure adequate and competent medical care in a remote, rural area."[12] Other statements by the office extend the same philosophy to other types of geographical areas. It would appear extremely unlikely that there will be change toward attacks on legitimate transactions without either substantial advance notice or new legislation.

HOSPITAL–BASED PHYSICIAN AGREEMENTS

The recruitment procedures for hospital-based and nonhospital-based physicians are similar. Many of the planning and implementation steps we have outlined in previous chapters apply as well to the recruitment of anesthesiologists, directors of pathology departments, radiologists, directors of emergency rooms, and so on. The primary difference between recruiting a hospital-based physician and a nonhospital-based physician is in the steps involved in determining need and in the need for financial assistance.

If a hospital is losing its director of the pathology department, there is clearly a need for a replacement. In this case, the extensive tables used to determine the number of physicians necessary per population are not applicable. However, if the hospital is considering the establishment of a new department that requires a hospital-based physician as a director, the hospital would be well-advised to perform an indepth marketing analysis to determine the future success of that department.

Another difference between recruiting a hospital-based and a nonhospital-based physician is in the offering of financial arrangements. In many cases, a hospital-based physician contracts with the hospital and receives a predetermined financial package. Office space and office personnel are not always a consideration.

The guidelines in Appendix 6–A, prepared by the American Hospital Association, can assist in the development of a contractual agreement with a hospital-based physician. Once the financial arrangements have been defined and put into a contractual form, the recruitment process can continue.

NOTES

1. National Center for Health Statistics, "More Empty Beds at Most Hospitals," *Hospital Progress,* October 1981, p. 79. (Advertisement of American Medical Buildings)

2. Jean T. Settlemyer, Administrator, Glen R. Frye Memorial Hospital, Hickory, North Carolina, 1980: personal communication.

3. Emanuel Tanay, "Society is Getting the Doctor it Deserves," *Medical Economics,* June 14, 1976, p. 107.

4. Michael Hackman of the law firm of Lewitt, Hackman, Hoefflin, and Shapiro of Encino, California, contributed substantially to this section.

5. *CCH Medicare and Medicaid Guide 1977, Transfer Binder* (Chicago: Commerce Clearinghouse, 1977), #28-443.

6. *CCH Medicare and Medicaid Guide 1978, Transfer Binder* (Chicago: Commerce Clearinghouse, 1978), #29-091.

7. *Public Law, 95-142,* Oct. 25, 1977, 91 Stat 1175.

8. *CCH Medicare and Medicaid Guide, Medicare and Medicaid Amendments of 1980* (Chicago: Commerce Clearinghouse, 1980), vol. 3, sec. 917, paragraphs b(1)-b(2).

9. *CCH Medicare and Medicaid Guide, 1980,* vol. 3, sec. 1877 (B)(3)(b).

10. *Ibid.,* vol. 3, sec. 1877, paragraph 17, 097.

11. Correspondence with the Office of Program Integrity, 1978–1980.

12. Don Nicholson, Director, Office of Program Integrity, Department of Health, Education and Welfare, in correspondence with HEW Secretary Joseph Califano, 1978.

Appendix 6–A

American Hospital Association Guidelines for Establishing Contractual Relationships between Hospitals and Physicians

PREFATORY NOTE

These guidelines are applicable primarily to contractual arrangements between a hospital and those physicians who direct its diagnostic and/or therapeutic departments. If a hospital desires to use the sample contract to define relationships with other physicians, each provision should be examined carefully for its applicability to specific situations. The guidelines are *not* intended in any way to apply to agreements with house staff in approved graduate medical education programs.

INTRODUCTION

The American Hospital Association believes that the policy decision to enter into contractual relationships with physicians to establish an exclusive practice within the hospital should preferably be implemented only after full deliberative discussion with and the support of appropriate representatives of the medical staff.*

The American Hospital Association believes that any institutional arrangement with a physician should be fair to the parties involved, should be conducive to excellence of medical care, and should promote the interests of the patient and of the community served by the institution. The Association

---

*Appropriate medical staff representatives cannot be specified in these guidelines because each hospital has its own methods of working with medical staff. For example, medical staff representation can be provided by physician members of the governing board, the executive committee of the medical staff, the professional relations committee, or through the joint conference committee. Local situations will determine the best choice.

Source: Reprinted with the permission of the American Hospital Association, ©1976.

emphasizes the necessity to give full consideration to the interests of the community in recognition of the institution's accountability to the public.

Social, economic, and political pressures resulting from increasing health care costs and from increasing sophistication of the public are directed toward increased efficiency and economy of health care in the United States. The American Hospital Association does not recommend any one pattern of provision of hospital or medical services, and suggests that there should be experimentation with and demonstration of different patterns of providing high-quality health care, so that the United States can be assured of progressive developments and proper adjustments to changing times. There must be flexibility in an institution's financial relationships with physicians. The nation is too large and the problems are too complex and varied to permit rigid or unrealistic limitations and arrangements.

GENERAL POLICIES

1. The American Hospital Association recognizes that good medical care is being provided in hospitals by physicians under many forms of mutual agreement.

2. The American Hospital Association believes it is the right and responsibility of hospitals to develop with physicians contractual terms on the basis of local conditions and needs that are fair to patients and support the provision of high-quality care.

3. Every physician in the hospital is expected to exercise freely and completely, within the framework of medical staff bylaws, his medical judgment and skill and to strive constantly to promote improvement in the quality of medical care. All medical practice is subject to continuing review by the medical staff organization.
   The practice of a physician under contract should be, from the standpoint of medical judgment, as independent as that of any other physician. As a potential member of the hospital medical staff subject to its bylaws, rules, and regulations, his qualifications should be determined and approved by the medical staff and the governing board according to the usual procedures applicable to all physicians granted privileges in the hospital.

4. Certain diagnostic and therapeutic services are a vital part of professional services provided in a hospital. A hospital should provide what the attending physicians need for diagnosis and treatment of their patients. These needs include space, facilities, and equipment and trained personnel in operating rooms, delivery rooms, medical and surgical wards, and laboratory, x-ray, and other diagnostic and therapeutic areas. The range of professional services and the skilled personnel necessary to provide them

in a hospital shall be determined in accordance with the institution's by-laws and policies, with due consideration being given to the financial and manpower resources of the hospital and to the availability of community resources.

5. Whenever a contractual relationship establishes an exclusive practice within the hospital, it is recommended that the governing authority of the institution seek the advice of appropriate medical staff representatives before it approves the schedule of charges for the professional component of the services provided.

6. A physician under contract is entitled to fair and equitable remuneration for his services. Factors to be considered include training and experience, time and talent, responsibilities for supervision, participation in education programs, level of compensation prevailing in the locality for physicians of comparable qualifications, and difficulty of the procedures and functions carried out.

7. As diagnostic, treatment, and other services become more complex, consultations with the appropriate medical staff representatives should be held on matters relating to hospital-physician relationships. These consultations should cover not only the original selection of the contracting physician, but also any issue that may arise concerning charges to patients, compensation, staffing and equipping of the department, quality and accessibility of departmental services, and the health and safety of patients and personnel.

8. Physician contracts should be reviewed by the administration and the contracting physician on a regular basis, preferably annually, to ensure that the terms of the agreement, professional and administrative, are being fulfilled. If warranted in the judgment of either the contracting physician or the administration, the contract may be subjected to further review by appropriate representatives of the governing board and/or the medical staff.

9. Physician contracts should provide for orderly resolution of any disputes that may arise and involve appropriate medical staff representatives in such resolutions. (See the footnote on page 76 concerning "appropriate medical staff representatives.")

THE CONTRACTING PHYSICIAN'S ADMINISTRATIVE RESPONSIBILITIES

Although the administrative responsibilities of a physician under contract might be clearly differentiated in theory from his medical care role as a physician, they are not easy to differentiate in practice, because they exist and operate simultaneously. As a physician, he must be responsive to the medical staff organization for his activities as a practitioner. In the administrative relationship, a physician must be responsive to the hospital administration for abiding by the administrative regulations of the hospital. In addition, when the physician is head of a department, he is responsible to the hospital administration for providing information regarding the needs of his department, for assisting in the development of administrative regulations as they pertain to his department, and for cooperating with the administration in the effective management of the hospital. The hospital should require the same economical and efficient operation of a department headed by a physician as that expected of other departments of the hospital and must have administrative control over departments headed by physicians comparable to its administrative control over all other departments.

When a physician is to serve as the head of a diagnostic and/or therapeutic department of the hospital, a specific contractual agreement with that physician may be appropriate.* Through this contract, the hospital should retain certain authority to ensure appropriate services to patients and effective operation of the department.

CONTRACTS WITH PHYSICIANS

It is important that legal advice be obtained before a hospital enters into a contract with a physician. Apart from ensuring that the contract conforms to the parties' intentions, legal advice will be helpful to ensure that local law and regulations are complied with and to avoid unintended and incidental effects of the contract, such as those affecting the status of the physician as an independent contractor or an employee. The formal relationship between the hospital and a physician under contract should:

1. Be entered into only after careful consideration of the full impact on the cost and quality of patient care.

   Comment: The agreement should stipulate that rates and charges made for services that appear on a patient's hospital bill are fair and reasonable and in keeping with the schedule of rates and charges approved by the hospital. The same principle should be followed when the physician sub-

---

*A contractual agreement is not necessary or appropriate in all instances. For example, in the case of an uncompensated physician department head, responsibilities and authority of the position can often be effectively expressed through corporate bylaws or medical staff bylaws and regulations.

mits separate bills. These rates and charges should be subject to periodic review and evaluation.†

2. Provide for periodic review by the appropriate body of the medical staff of the quality, appropriateness, and adequacy of professional service provided by the physician under contract.

Comment: Physicians under contract as members of the medical staff should have their professional activities and the maintenance of their professional competence periodically reviewed by their professional colleagues in the same manner as other members of the medical staff.

3. Provide that the determination of all administrative standards is a responsibility of hospital administration consistent with policy guidelines set by the governing board.

Comment: Physicians under contract are accountable to the administration of the hospital for the proper management of their departments. Employees in departments headed by physicians under contract are accountable in the same manner as employees in all other departments.

4. Provide for proper coordination with the other services and departments of the hospital.

Comment: In order to ensure coordination, the administrative policies and procedures of the hospital should be uniformly binding on all departments involved in the operation of the hospital.

5. Enable hospital administration to retain control over the personnel program for all employees working in the hospital.

Comment: Personnel policies and procedures, including wage and salary administration, should be uniformly applied to all employees working in the hospital.

6. Enable hospital administration to retain usual direction and control over the personnel and material resources to be available for the rendering of services.

Comment: The hospital should operate in an efficient manner by using judiciously the available resources to maintain the standards of performance that have been adopted by the hospital in consultation with the physician under contract. The physician should participate in the approval of standards for the selection of supplies and equipment in the same manner as other department directors.

†See number 8 above.

7. Specify the responsibilities of the hospital and the physician in relation to the hospital's training and educational programs and to educational programs designed to enhance the physician's professional competence.

   Comment: Policies should be outlined, at least in general terms, to delineate the physician's part in support of in-hospital programs as well as the hospital's responsibility to provide opportunities for the physician to become the beneficiary of educational activities.

8. Anticipate and resolve in advance, insofar as practicable, any issues that might otherwise be unresolved and open to dispute or controversy.

9. Permit hospitals that so desire to contract with professional associations or corporations organized by physicians for the practice of medicine. There would appear to be no basic disadvantage to hospitals in contracting with such associations or corporations so long as (1) the agreement designates the physician or physicians who are to be personally responsible for performance of services and who must qualify and be approved for medical staff membership; (2) each designated physician personally signs the agreement with the hospital and the association or corporation and agrees, jointly and severally with the association or corporation, to accept responsibility for the performance of the services; (3) the addition of any physician, substitution of any successor physician, or designation of any temporary replacement physician is subject to the approval of the hospital, just as in contracting with individual physicians; (4) the effect of the agreement is substantially the same as if the hospital were contracting solely with the physician or physicians who are to perform the services; (5) the hospital reserves the right to terminate the agreement in the event of the death, disability, loss of professional qualification or nonperformance by one or more designated physicians, or the transfer of equity in the association or corporation that is not approved by the hospital, in addition to any other grounds of termination; and (6) in addition to usual legal consultation, special legal and accountancy advice is obtained to ensure that the contract arrangement does not unintentionally penalize or artificially reduce reimbursement from third-party payers that would otherwise properly be due. Physicians should have sole responsibility for the determination that compliance with these conditions would be consistent with their intended fringe benefit or organizational purposes. Appropriate documents should also be prepared in the event of addition or substitution of any physician or any other modification of the agreement.

   Sample contractual arrangements and alternative approaches to compensation are discussed below.

SAMPLE CONTRACTUAL ARRANGEMENT

As a guide for hospitals that wish to arrange a contractual agreement with a physician, a group, or a professional association or corporation, the American Hospital Association offers the following sample agreement. It is emphasized, however, that this agreement is only a suggested sample and must be adapted by the hospitals and physicians using it, with the advice of legal counsel, in order to properly provide for local circumstances and individual attitudes.

SAMPLE AGREEMENT

THIS AGREEMENT, made and executed in duplicate at (city) _____ (state) _____ as of _____, 19 _____, by and between _____ HOSPITAL, a corporation,* hereinafter referred to as "Hospital," and _____, M.D., hereinafter referred to as "Physician."

WITNESSETH:

WHEREAS, the Hospital is the owner and operator of a hospital at (city) _____, (state) _____, in which there is located a department of _____, and

WHEREAS, the Physician is qualified to practice _____ medicine in the state of _____ and has met the requirements for membership on the _____† medical staff, and

WHEREAS, the parties desire to provide a full statement of their agreement in connection with the operation of said department of _____ in the Hospital during the term of this contract.

THEREFORE, in consideration of the mutual covenants and agreements of this contract, it is understood and agreed by and between the parties hereto as follows:

FIRST: The Physician, upon recommendation of the medical staff and appointment by the governing authority of the hospital, and by virtue of this agreement, is, or within _____ days must qualify as, a member of the _____† medical staff of the Hospital, with all of the privileges and subject to all the responsibilities of _____† medical staff membership, and subject to the professional supervision of the executive committee of the

---

*Use proper descriptive terminology, such as corporation, trust, and so forth.

†Insert appropriate category such as courtesy, associate, active, and so forth.

medical staff. It is expressly agreed that continuation of this agreement shall be dependent on the Physician's continued membership on the medical staff of the Hospital (and, unless the Physician was previously a member of the medical staff, his membership on that staff and all clinical privileges shall terminate if this agreement is terminated).

> *Comment:* The material within parentheses would be an option applicable only when the physician is to receive an appointment on an exclusive or shared exclusive basis. Applicability of the option and its terms should be specifically discussed with legal counsel.

SECOND: The Physician shall serve as the professional and administrative head of the Hospital's Department or Section of _____. In his administrative relationships, the Physician is under the direction of the chief executive officer and shall be responsible to the hospital administration for abiding by the administrative regulations of the Hospital. In addition, he shall be responsible to the hospital administration for providing information regarding the budgetary and other needs of his department, for assisting in the development of administrative regulations as they pertain to his department, and for cooperating with the administration in the effective management of the department.

THIRD: The Hospital shall make available during the term of the contract the space designated for the department of _____, and, in addition, the Hospital shall make available such equipment as mutually agreed to as necessary for the proper operation and conduct of the department. The Hospital shall also keep and maintain said equipment in good order and repair. The Hospital shall furnish the department with utilities, housekeeping, laundry, and other services as may be required for the proper operation and conduct of the department.

> *Comment:* This provision sets forth that the hospital assumes responsibility for purchase and maintenance of all equipment. Patently, the hospital's decision should be made in consultation with the physician in charge of the department in question and must always be made in accordance with an effective planning program and recognition of the hospital's responsibility for the quality of care received by its patients and for the prudent expenditure of health care resources.

FOURTH: The Hospital shall purchase all necessary expendable supplies for the proper operation of the department.

FIFTH: All nonmedical personnel required for the proper operation of the department of _____ shall be employed or assigned by the Hospital, after consultation with the Physician. Salaries, benefits, and personnel policies applicable to persons employed in the department shall be uniform with those of other Hospital employees in similar personnel classifications.

SIXTH: In operating the department of _____ at the Hospital, and serving as its (director, head, and so forth) _____, the Physician shall devote his best ability to its proper management and shall use the assigned premises solely for the practice of (specify service) _____.

Comment: A pertinent provision should include a stipulation concerning how the department is to be supervised and the professional services to be rendered during the physician's absence.

Under certain conditions the parties may wish to add one of these sentences:

• The Physician shall confine his practice to the Hospital except when practice at other institutions or locations is agreed to by the governing board of the Hospital in an appropriate document.

• The Physician shall confine his practice of _____ to the Hospital under the terms of this contract and shall not provide _____ services at any other location.

Or the parties also may wish to set forth additional specific items relative to practice in other locations.

Hospitals are urged to give careful consideration when a physician or a group of physicians under contract seeks to practice also at other institutions. Sharing services in this manner may be the only way that service can be provided in many smaller hospitals. In some cases it may also be necessary in larger hospitals. It is also recognized that sharing services could lead to neglect of one or both hospitals. Periodic review and the inclusion of a clause for contract cancellation should provide adequate control of possible abuse.

SEVENTH: The Physician shall participate for reasonable periods of time in the educational programs conducted by the Hospital and shall perform such other teaching functions within the Hospital as are necessary to ensure the Hospital's compliance with requirements of accrediting bodies.

Comment: A full-time physician should have reasonable opportunity to attend appropriate scientific meetings. This section of the agreement, accordingly, might be enlarged to specify that financial provisions for travel and professional development for the physician will be agreed to annually and included in the departmental budget.

EIGHTH: The Physician and the employees under his supervision shall comply with the policies, rules, and regulations of the Hospital.

NINTH: The Physician agrees to perform all (specify) _____ services required in the care (or examination) of hospital patients, hospital employees, applicants for employment, and hospital students. Charges shall be reduced or waived for professional services to the extent and in proportion to the degree that hospital charges are reduced or waived for any reason for (1) patients, including but not limited to indigency, pursuit of research and special studies, and courtesy; (2) students of the hospital; (3) applicants for hospital employment; (4) employees injured or afflicted within the scope of their employment (to the extent to which the charge must be borne by the Hospital or the employee); and (5) employees, in accordance with hospital personnel policies.

Comment: It is assumed that the basis of compensation will take into consideration the usual charges that would be made for nonchargeable services. If desired, the parties may include the value of such services with actual billings for chargeable services and adjust the basis of compensation accordingly.

TENTH: The Hospital shall approve a schedule of any amounts to be charged to patients for the professional component of services rendered in the Hospital's department of _____. Before establishing or modifying such charges, the Hospital shall seek the counsel and written recommendations of the Physician.* The amounts to be charged patients for services rendered in the Hospital's department of _____ shall include the Hospital's cost of maintaining the department and shall include as an element the Physician's compensation for professional and administrative services.

ELEVENTH: The Physician shall file with the Hospital a record of all services rendered to patients in the department of _____. The Hospital shall collect the charges for these services at the same time as charges owed by said patients for other services are collected.†

Comment: If desired by the physician, this paragraph may include, as the final sentence, "The Hospital shall indicate on its billhead the name and title of the Physician."†

TWELFTH: On or before the _____ day of each month, the Hospital shall present to the Physician a statement of gross income and expense pertaining to the operation of the department of _____ during the preceding month.

---

*Where an exclusive practice contract is involved, see page 80, number 5.

†See also page 87, related to direct billing to patients.

THIRTEENTH: The Physician's compensation for professional services shall be fixed as follows:

Seven alternatives are presented below. It should be noted that many other alternatives exist that may be appropriate under some circumstances. (Whatever provisions are determined through negotiations to be mutually agreeable should be inserted here.)

Alternative 1. Salary

An amount of $_____ payable in installments at intervals of _____.

Alternative 2. Percentage of Net Departmental Income

From the total of reconciled departmental charges for said preceding calendar month, the Hospital shall deduct _____ percent relative to inpatient services and _____ percent relative to outpatient services as allowances for departmental bad debts. There shall also be deducted all costs incurred pursuant to paragraphs THIRD, FOURTH, and FIFTH hereof. Of the remaining amount, _____ percent shall be the Physician's compensation, which shall be paid over to him with the monthly statement of gross income and expense provided for by paragraph TWELFTH herein. The remainder thereof shall be retained by the Hospital as reimbursement for the cost of hospital services. The above percentages for departmental bad debts shall be adjusted every six months in order to reflect the record of bad debts for the previous six-month period, based upon the collection experienced for that period.

Alternative 3. Percentage of Net Departmental Income with Sliding Scale

From the total of reconciled departmental charges for the preceding calendar month, the Hospital shall deduct _____ percent relative to inpatient services and _____ percent relative to outpatient services as allowances for departmental bad debts. There shall also be deducted all costs incurred pursuant to paragraphs THIRD, FOURTH, and FIFTH hereof. Of the remaining amount, the Physician's compensation, which shall be paid over to him with the monthly statement of gross income and expense provided for by paragraph TWELFTH herein, shall be computed on the basis of the following percentages.

1. _____ percent of the first $_____

2. _____ percent of the next $_____

3. _____ percent of the amount above $_____

The remainder of said charges shall be retained by the Hospital as reimbursement for the cost of hospital services. The percentages allowed for departmental bad debts shall be adjusted every six months in order to reflect the record of bad debts for the previous six-month period, based upon the collection experience for that period.

Alternative 4. Percentage of Adjusted Gross Departmental Billings

From the total of reconciled departmental charges for the preceding calendar month, the Hospital shall deduct _____ percent relative to inpatient services and _____ percent relative to outpatient services as allowances for departmental bad debts. Of the remaining amount, _____ percent shall be the Physician's compensation, which shall be paid over to the Physician with the monthly statement of gross income and expense provided by paragraph TWELFTH herein. The remainder thereof shall be retained by the Hospital as reimbursement for the cost of hospital services. The percentages allowed for bad debts shall be adjusted every six months in order to reflect the record of departmental bad debts for the previous six-month period, based upon the collection experience for that period.

Alternative 5. Percentage of Adjusted Gross with Maximum Limit

From the total of reconciled departmental charges for the preceding calendar month, the Hospital shall deduct _____ percent relative to inpatient services and _____ percent relative to outpatient services as allowances for departmental bad debts. Of the remaining amount, _____ percent, up to a maximum of $_____, shall be the Physician's compensation, which shall be paid over to him with the monthly statement of gross income and expense provided for by paragraph TWELFTH herein. The remainder thereof shall be retained by the Hospital as reimbursement for the cost of hospital services. The percentages allowed for bad debts shall be adjusted every six months in order to reflect the record of departmental bad debts for the previous six-month period, based upon the collection experience for that period.

Alternative 6. Direct Billing to Patients

As the sole source of compensation hereunder, the Physician shall look exclusively to his patients, or those persons or third-party payers responsible for their services, in accordance with charges approved under paragraph TENTH herein. Charges shall be reduced or waived to the extent provided under paragraph NINTH herein.

> *Comment:* When Alternative 6 is used, appropriate modification must be made to the second sentence of paragraph ELEVENTH. If billing service is to be provided by the hospital, it will be necessary to indicate the scope and method of service and how the expense of the service is to be borne.

See Types of Arrangements for Compensation and the discussion of billing arrangements under subhead 4, Cost per Unit of Service.

Alternative 7. Fee for Physician's Service Combined with Hospital Billing

As the sole source of compensation hereunder, the Physician shall accept fees for services from patients, or those persons or third-party payers responsible for their services, in accordance with charges approved under paragraph TENTH herein. Approval of these fees for services are to be negotiated separately from the Hospital's determination of charges for services necessary to cover the Hospital's cost of maintaining the department, even though the Physician's fees and the Hospital's cost may be reflected in a single charge to the patient computed on the basis of each unit of service. Fee-for-service charges will be reduced or waived by the Physician to the extent provided under paragraph NINTH herein.

Comment: When Alternative 7 is used, a fee for each unit of service and the number of units per service shall be agreed to by the physician and approved by the hospital. Compensation to the physician shall usually be his unit fee multiplied by the units of service rendered in a stipulated time frame to be more particularly described in the contract or in the approved schedule of units per service. Any changes from time to time in aggregate charge to the patient may result from a change in the hospital's service charge, the physician's fee or schedule of units, or a combination of these factors.

Comment: The American Hospital Association believes that the physician should be properly compensated, and that by taking into account the level of compensation of other physicians in the community, the comparability of the training and experience of those physicians, regional economic factors, the demands that will be made on the physician's time, the complexity of the services to be performed, and the degree of expertise required, the amount of compensation considered proper and equitable by both hospital and physician can be translated into a salary, a percentage, or other arrangement.

As examples, seven alternative financial arrangements are listed in the sample agreement. This list is by no means exhaustive. Other, fundamentally different types of arrangements are possible, and all may be proper providing they are mutually satisfactory, do not result in exploitation of the patient, the hospital, or the physician, and are not at variance with applicable laws. (See Types of Arrangements for Compensation.)

The seven alternative arrangements are themselves amenable to whatever modifications may be deemed desirable locally. For instance, alternative arrangements 4 and 5 provide for a percentage of "adjusted" gross as the physician's compensation: that is, the actual gross is reduced by an amount representing bad debts before the percentage is applied. However, a hospital might prefer to use the actual gross departmental income against which to apply an appropriately computed percentage factor. The stipulation of a maximum, set forth in alternative arrangement 5, may be included in any provision concerning the physician's compensation. Similarly, the sliding scale schedule that is an element of alternative arrangement 3 may be appropriately included in any provision involving a percentage arrangement. Also, if a maximum is to be fixed, the hospital might give consideration to establishing a minimum compensation for the physician.

Certain combinations of the alternatives listed are also feasible. For example, the hospital might wish to provide a fixed salary or stipend as compensation for the physician's administrative activities as department head, and concomitantly to provide a percentage arrangement, or separate billing on a fee-for-service basis, to compensate for the physician's professional services. The salary in such an arrangement should relate to the time and talent required for administrative duties. The concomitant percentage or fee should not exploit either party. When salary is the only method of compensation, the physician should be entitled to the normal fringe benefits prevailing in the hospital.

FOURTEENTH: As a member of the medical staff, the Physician will cooperate with and assist other members of the staff in preparation of clinical reports for publication and will use his efforts to elevate the performance of the Hospital staff in the field of medical science.

FIFTEENTH: The Physician shall be present in the Hospital and shall consult with staff physicians in proper cases, during such hours as the Hospital shall determine to be necessary and proper. If the approval of the Hospital is obtained in writing, the work of the Physician may be done in part by such other physician(s) as may be duly appointed to the medical staff by the Hospital. Nothing contained in this paragraph or in this agreement shall be construed to permit assignment of any rights under this agreement, and such assignment is expressly prohibited.

Comment: This provision makes reference to augmentation of the physician staff, when such is recommended by the physician. A hospital might wish to enlarge this paragraph by including a provision that the physician must arrange for professional assistance when, in the opinion of those concerned, the executive committee of the medical staff and administration, the proper care of patients requires that the work load of the physician be shared with additional physicians. Both parties to any contract or agreement should be aware that if the work load increases sufficiently, additional physician(s) must be brought into the department.

SIXTEENTH: In the performance of the work, duties, and obligations devolving upon him under this agreement, it is mutually understood and agreed that the Physician is at all times acting and performing as an independent contractor practicing his profession of medicine and surgery and specializing in _____. The Hospital shall neither have nor exercise any control or direction over the methods by which the Physician or physician employees under his control shall perform their work and functions; the sole interest and responsibility of the Hospital is to ensure that the Department of _____ and services covered by this agreement shall be performed and rendered in a competent, efficient, and satisfactory manner. The standards of medical practice and professional duties of the Physician shall be determined by the medical staff of the Hospital. All applicable provisions of law and other rules and regulations of any and all governmental authorities relating to licensure and regulation of physicians and hospitals and to the operation of the department shall be fully complied with by all parties hereto; in addition, the parties shall also operate and conduct the department in accordance with (optional: the standards and recommendations of the Joint Commission on Accreditation of Hospitals), the bylaws of the Hospital, and the bylaws, rules, and regulations of the medical staff as may be in effect from time to time.

Comment: The above paragraph would not be applicable in the case of a contract with a physician who is an employee of the hospital. It is intended to document and support the position of the hospital when the physician is intended to be an "independent contractor" rather than an employee. It can be important in many areas of law where the distinction is critical. For example, it may be helpful to demonstrate that the physician is not an employee for workmen's compensation purposes and for certain tax and employment benefit purposes. For liability purposes it can help establish that, if the hospital itself exercised due care in selecting the physician as an independent contractor, the hospital will not be liable for any of his negligent acts or omissions in performing under the contract.

This provision should be carefully considered with legal counsel, along with all other provisions of the contract and actual practices by the hospital and the physician. All contractual provisions and practices should be consistent with one another and local law. If a court is convinced that the physician is controlled in his judgment and discretion to the extent of an employee, the court may be inclined to disregard the above provision. Legal counsel can be helpful in suggesting precautions to be followed in performance that will tend to support recognition of the intended relationship. Although results cannot be guaranteed, the effort merits serious consideration.

SEVENTEENTH: This agreement shall remain in full force and effect for a term of _____ year(s) from and after (date of contract) _____, and for successive terms of like duration unless either party shall, within _____ days of termination of the original or any successive term, give written notice of the party's intention to terminate the agreement at the conclusion of the term then in the progress.

Comment: According to the preference of the parties, the term of the agreement may be for a stated term, for a series of successive terms unless notice of termination is given, and so forth. Care should be taken to avoid a desired term that may be abrogated as a practical matter by a period of notice of termination by either party. Legal consultation should be obtained as to appropriate provisions to be inserted relating to termination by either party for cause.

IN WITNESS WHEREOF, the Hospital has caused this agreement to be executed and its corporate seal to be hereunto affixed by its duly authorized officers, and the Physician has executed this agreement by hereunto setting his hand as of the day and year first above written.

_____
Physician

_____
Hospital

By _____

ATTEST:

TYPES OF ARRANGEMENTS FOR COMPENSATION

The hospital-physician arrangements for compensation most frequently encountered are briefly discussed in the following paragraphs. There are many possible modifications or combinations of these arrangements. The advantages or disadvantages referred to are not necessarily universal. What works well in one hospital might be a poor arrangement for another hospital or another physician. Conversely, the generally recognized disadvantages of a certain arrangement might not pertain in a specific situation. The chief executive officer, the medical staff, the board of trustees, and the physician involved must determine the relative merits or deficiencies of each arrangement on the basis of what is best for them and especially for the patients they serve.

1. Salary

Payment of a salary is an uncomplicated arrangement for a physician's compensation. Perquisites such as vacations with pay, pensions, annuities, and protection of income during prolonged illness are easily provided for in a salary arrangement. Provision of a salary may be the only way to guarantee a satisfactory income for the physician or to attract a physician to a certain locality. The hospital, and the physician as well, may find the salary arrangement the least cumbersome of the alternative arrangements described when the work load of the department involved indicates the need for an additional member on its professional staff.

Many physicians under contract find the salary arrangement to be convenient, satisfactory, and completely acceptable. Salary arrangements need not interpose a third party between the patient and the physician or decrease personal incentive. Certainly a salary arrangement between a hospital and a physician produces no third-party interference with the professional judgment of the physician concerning the care of the patient. Some may fault a salary arrangement as lacking an incentive to productivity. The desire to provide optimal care of patients motivates the majority of physicians. In medicine there are effective incentives other than financial ones.

2. Percentage of Net Departmental Income

A negotiated percentage of net departmental income can be turned over to the physician as his compensation. This arrangement requires sophisticated accounting practices and procedures. If such are in effect, the arrangement ensures that all pertinent hospital expenses are provided for before the computation of the physician's compensation is made; that is, it ensures that the department will not inadvertently be subsidized by other income-producing activities of the hospital. But even when good cost-finding and accounting procedures are employed, there are opportunities for dispute concerning the propriety of certain charges against the cost of operating the department. It is true, of course, that an improper charge to departmental expense would unjustly reduce the income of the physician.

Some hospitals prefer the percentage-of-net arrangement because it provides an incentive to the physician for economy in the use of supplies and personnel. Conversely, however, some hospitals reason that the physician might be influenced, perhaps subconsciously, by such an arrangement to fail to recommend hospital expenditures that would improve patient care because the resultant increase in expense would reduce the net departmental income on which his personal income is based.

3. Percentage of Gross Departmental Charges

A percentage of gross departmental charges or percentage of adjusted gross departmental income (adjusted for uncollectible accounts receivable and perhaps also for discounted billings to indigent patients, employees, or others) is a relatively uncomplicated arrangement on which to base a physician's compensation. It avoids problems of judgment in the allocation of expense items to the department. The compensation of the physician, if computed on the basis of this arrangement, bears a direct relationship to the work load of his department. This arrangement, however, provides no incentive to the physician for effecting economies, and it brings about the rather incongruous situation in which any increase in pertinent charges to patients, even when made solely to cover increased departmental operating expenses, accrues to a considerable extent to the financial benefit of the physician.

The American Hospital Association does not recommend any particular percentage of either gross or net departmental income as the proper share for the physician. There are, of course, numerous variable factors to be considered, such as the level of charges to patients, the cost of departmental operations, and the training and experience of the physician. Both of the percentage arrangements are likely to present difficulties when the volume of departmental work requires augmentation of the professional staff, especially when an assistant is to be compensated out of the portion of departmental income turned over to the physician serving as the department head. Many hospitals have experienced significant annual increases in the number of x-ray and laboratory services, with no increase in bed complement. As the volume of services provided by a department increases, the personal income of the physician involved increases concomitantly and commensurately, unless either the charges to patients or the percentages are reduced. As the volume of work increases and additional professional personnel become necessary, understandably the physician may be reluctant to accept the reduction in his personal income necessary to provide compensation for an additional colleague. Thus, under a percentage arrangement, a busy department may be permitted to continue understaffed with professional personnel, to the detriment of patient care, unless the safeguard of annual review is carefully adhered to.

4. Cost per Unit of Service (percentage of net on a per unit basis)

The cost per unit of service arrangement permits the hospital to exercise complete control over the personnel and administrative practices of the particular department. The total of hospital expenses involved, including indirect expenses, is translated into a hospital cost per unit of service or per procedure. The physician establishes and charges fees to patients and periodically pays the hospital the total of its expenses computed by multiplying the cost per unit of service or procedure by the number of units or number of procedures.

This arrangement provides that the physician charge patients for hospital services. Accordingly, as part of this type of arrangement, the hospital should require that it serve as the billing and collecting agent for the physician, the expenses of this function being included in the reimbursable cost, and should require that the governing authority of the hospital approve the schedule of fees to be charged patients. Such an arrangement also should provide for semiannual or annual retroactive adjustments of the cost reimbursement amounts paid to or retained by the hospital to take care of underpayment or overpayment brought about by fluctuations in volume of cases or procedures or by unusual fluctuations in the hospital's expenses.

As in the case of percentage of net departmental income, the cost per unit of service arrangement may result in differences of opinion concerning specific charges to departmental expense.

5. Combination of Minimum Guarantee and Other Method of Compensation

It will sometimes be useful to combine the basic method of compensation, on the basis of either a percentage of net or gross departmental charges or direct billing by the physician himself, with a guarantee to ensure that this method of determining compensation will produce a minimum, agreed-upon rate of compensation to the physician for a stated period of time. Such a combination may be of particular interest when a new service is being instituted under an existing contract, and its volume has not been determined. Typically, the compensation realized under the basic method of compensation will be set off periodically against any advancements toward the agreed-upon rate guaranteed by the hospital. It should be recognized that the basic compensation may fluctuate, so that any advancement of the guarantee may be made from time to time. Also, arrangements should be made for a review at intervals or at the conclusion of the guarantee period to offset any excess of advancement of guarantee against the basic compensation paid to the physician in any intervals of the guarantee period. The hospital will want to ensure that the guarantee arrangement is consistent with reimbursement policies of third-party payers so that it can avoid or reduce any nonallowance of the guarantee for reimbursement purposes. The hospital will also wish to ensure, through its legal counsel, that it has corporate authority, or authority as a public body, to enter into such a guarantee arrangement.

6. Lease

A lease or concession arrangement is, in the view of the American Hospital Association, generally not desirable. There may be legal prohibitions against such arrangements in the case of government-owned (county, district, or municipal) hospitals. In many states a voluntary nonprofit hospital may risk loss of all or part of its ad valorem (property) tax exemption if it leases facilities to a physician under contract for the latter's profit. Even when there is no actual leasehold, a lease type of concession arrangement, such as the so-called "mutual working agreement," involves the possible loss of effective administrative coordination or control of services.

Many hospitals have considered adopting a lease arrangement with physicians to avoid any liability for professional conduct of the lessee-physician. In many instances, and in a number of states, a lease arrangement with a properly selected and qualified lessee-physician will have that effect, but there is no guarantee that this incidental aspect of a lease arrangement will be recognized by the courts in every situation. Thus, the hospital's desire for insulation from any liability for the lessee-physician's professional acts or omissions should be balanced with all other factors relating to the most desirable arrangement.

Even if a lease agreement would insulate the hospital from liability within its state, that alone would not necessarily be sufficient to justify the lease approach. No matter how the professional services are to be rendered, the hospital will want to take steps to ensure that the quality of services is at least equal to those provided by physicians under personal contract. This means that the lessee-physician would be subject to the same standards and restrictions as if he were providing services under a professional contract.

As to availability of services, a lease type of arrangement frequently complicates replacement of the physician. Of special concern would be the problems associated with disability, death, and the administration of estates. In order to lease the department, assume the ownership of equipment, and meet payrolls, the replacement must be well financed through his own or other resources.

The hospital may also encounter a problem when it properly desires to retire or discharge a leaseholder who refuses to give up his lease, especially when a qualified and acceptable physician is not immediately available to assume the professional and financial burden of the lease arrangement. If the employees of the department involved are employees of the physician, they may become unemployed if the physician for any reason terminates his arrangement with the hospital. Obviously, this loss of personnel would endanger the continuity of services. Furthermore, if the employees of the department are the personal employees of the physician, with salary schedules, vacations, sick leave, and other employee benefits differing from those of the hospital's employees, there may well be a substantial cause for discord among hospital employees. If the physician also owned the equipment necessary for the provision of services, the disposition of departmental equipment owned by the physician could constitute a major problem upon his death, termination, or retirement.

Properly, the charges and income relative to essential hospital services are controlled by the hospital governing board, composed of persons expected to have no adverse financial interest in decisions concerning the hospital and the welfare of the patients. A lease arrangement could change this desirable pattern.

CHECKLIST FOR AGREEMENTS BETWEEN HOSPITALS AND PHYSICIANS

by James E. Ludlam, Esq.,
Musick, Peeler & Garrett, Los Angeles

Possible types of specialty

Radiology	CCU	Noninvasive cardiology
Pathology	ICU	Inhalation therapy
Emergency care	Cardiopulmonary	Medical director
EKG	Cardiorespiratory	Medical education
EEG	Physical therapy	Catheterization lab
Isotopes	Anesthesiology	Hemodialysis

Principal objectives of agreement

1. Fair and reasonable cost to patients

2. Assurance of quality

3. Mutual confidence within the triangle of specialist, medical staff, and administration

Preliminary information

1. State law and interpretations on the corporate practice of medicine

2. Existing arrangements in other departments

3. Expected volume—5-year projection

4. Open or closed department

5. Full-time or part-time

6. Number of specialists required and who should be responsible

7. Individual or corporate practice

8. What the service will do for the hospital in the future

9. Possible reimbursement problems

10. Problems relating to planning and to Section 221 of Public Law 92-603 as to service and capital expenditures

11. Availability of service elsewhere

12. Departmental responsibility with administrative and professional hierarchy

13. Space availability—immediate and future

14. State of the art as to capital equipment—potential functional obsolescence

15. Availability of specialists inside or outside the hospital and potential medical staff politics involved

16. Demand of medical staff for service

17. Availability of technical personnel

18. Cost factors, such as the budget and hospital costs for different levels and volumes of service

    a. Capital budget—determine best means of acquisition (purchase, lease, by hospital, by specialists, by gift, and so forth)

    b. Breakdown of direct and indirect costs (attempt to establish actual costs that are not specifically identified in the chart of accounts)

    c. Costs that can or cannot, at least in part, be controlled by the hospital, by the specialist, or by both (personnel costs may be primarily in control of the specialist, but space may not, while billing costs would be a hospital controllable item)

19. Expected patterns of charity allowances, discounts because of reimbursement, bad debts (inpatient and outpatient), and professional courtesy

20. Contract patterns in community, state, and nation

21. Net income necessary to recruit specialist(s) desired

22. Latest Internal Revenue Service (IRS), Workmen's Compensation, and Social Security Administration rulings on specialist agreements

23. Latest Joint Commission on Accreditation of Hospitals standards for the department or service

Types of arrangements to be considered

1. Salary

2. Percentage of gross

3. Percentage of modified gross

4. Percentage of net

5. Separate components for professional and technical administrative (hospital) activities

6. Complete separate billing and establishment of fees and charges

7. Any of above coupled with a guaranteed minimum

Deferred compensation potential

1. Plan approved by IRS applicable to hospital generally, such as a 402(b) annuity

2. Unapproved plan applicable to department only

3. Funded through a trust or insurance policy, or based solely on promise of hospital to pay

4. Insured or uninsured, and whether policy to be owned by hospital or specialist

5. Reimbursement implications both present and future

6. IRS implications for hospital and for physician

Fundamental contract provisions to be considered

1. Status of specialist as an independent contractor or as an employee

2. Designation of present and future space

3. Rights of specialist and hospital as to control of or consultation on purchase of capital equipment

4. Rights of specialist and hospital as to control of or consultation on quantity and brand of supplies

5. Method of employment and termination of technical personnel

6. Billing and accounting procedures, including types of reports and whether billing indicates name of specialist

7. Payments on cash or accrual basis, with provisions for bad debts

8. Rights of specialist to engage in outside practice

9. Rights of specialist regarding inhospital practice

10. Rights of outside consultants to use hospital space, equipment, and so forth

11. Allocation of losses on bad debts, charity, reimbursement, and professional courtesy (hospital, physician, or both)

12. Responsibility for teaching and research

13. Responsibility and compensation for services to hospital employees' medical needs (on job, off job, employment physicals, and so forth)

    a. Employee health insurance paid for by hospital or separately

    b. Covered by Workmen's Compensation

    c. Potential need for public liability insurance

14. Responsibility for control of quality

    a. Medical staff through appropriate committee

    b. Executive medical committee

    c. Joint conference committee

15. Responsibility for settlement of disputes

    a. Medical staff through appropriate committee

    b. Executive medical board

    c. Joint conference committee

    d. Arbitration

    e. Review by outside organization

    f. Right of representation by specialist

16. Right to terminate agreement

    a. By either party with or without cause on specified time of notice, such as 90 days

    b. By either party with specified cause, the cause being defined in agreement

    c. By either party after recommendation of executive committee of medical staff

    d. By hospital with concurrence of executive committee or joint conference committee

    e. Make agreement nonassignable and terminated automatically upon assignment

17. Term of agreement

    a. Indeterminate—terminable at will by either party

    b. Year to year

    c. Fixed term—automatically renewed unless terminated by prior notice

    d. Patient records remain property of hospital on termination

18. What happens in event of death or disability of specialist

    a. Automatically terminates

    b. Continues as to surviving partner or associates

    c. Rights of widow or widower must be limited to proceeds accrued prior to death unless a death allowance has been agreed to

19. Coverage

    a. Vague general statement, such as "usual or customary in the community"

    b. Specification of time of performance, such as 5 days per week, from 9 a.m. to 5 p.m., and so forth

    c. Performance subject to need for services as determined by executive committee or other appropriate medical staff committee

    d. Specification of vacation, leave, educational or meeting rights, and who pays costs of attendance

    e. Party responsible for coverage during absence and who pays for such coverage

    f. Anticipated requirement for additional professional coverage in event of expansion, increased work load, and so forth—may be related to dollar volume, number of procedures, or number of beds

20. Professional corporations

    a. Applicable IRS rulings

    b. Hospital may ignore the corporation and continue to deal with individuals, but this may create potential tax problems for the specialist

c. Requirement to designate an individual officer of corporation to be responsible to administration and medical staff

d. Rights of the hospital to terminate on death, retirement, or disability of designated individual, or change in control of corporation to avoid dealing with a stranger

e. Requirement that all stockholders be members of the medical staff

f. Billing in name of corporation or named individuals

g. Determination by physicians, with their tax counsel, whether amounts received by the professional corporation or association, under such conditions and other terms and relationships of the contract, may be considered as personal holding company income under Section 543 of the Internal Revenue Code

21. Requirement that all parties comply with state and federal laws, regulations, and so forth and with professional ethics or standards of designated professional organizations

22. Requirements for malpractice insurance, its limits, and who pays for it

23. Cross indemnities—evaluation by insurance carriers for all parties for possible adverse effects on premiums

Part II

Implementation of the Physician Recruitment Process—External Recruitment

After the financial considerations have been addressed, a budget prepared, and the contractual relationships agreed upon, the developmental phase of the physician recruitment process is complete. The implementation phase should now begin. This phase should concentrate on:

- establishment of the recruitment committee
- identification of physician sources
- determination of location preferences
- preinterviewing techniques
- interview and site visits
- follow-up, transition, and retention of the recruited physician

In the following six chapters, we will examine these aspects in the implementation phase of the external recruitment process. In Part III, we will deal with the establishment of the recruitment committee, retention of the active staff, and nonactive staff utilization in the implementation phase of the internal recruitment process.

Chapter 7

The External Recruitment Committee

The implementation phase of the recruitment program begins with the establishment of a physician recruitment committee. Regardless of what program option a hospital chooses, the recruitment committee members will have specific responsibilities and tasks to perform. The committee will be the active force that will locate the physician candidates, conduct the interviews, follow up on potential physician recruits, provide the basis for retaining the newly recruited physicians, and work with the outside firm if one is retained. The success or failure of the recruitment effort will many times depend on how well the recruitment committee performs these responsibilities.

RESPONSIBILITIES

The committee should consist of approximately six to ten members. One member should be the hospital administrator, and at least one other member should represent the governing board. The medical staff and community leaders should also be represented. If possible, the trustee and medical staff representatives should be the members who are on the planning committee. The community leader representatives could come from the areas of accounting, law, banking, business (the local chamber of commerce), education, industry, and religion. The committee could also include other health care providers, such as dentists, pharmacists and members of auxiliary and volunteer groups. In short, the committee members should be selected on the basis of their interest and support and provide a broad community foundation.

The degree of involvement of each committee member will depend on which program option the hospital chooses. Each option differs in terms of the degree of responsibility the hospital undertakes in relation to an outside recruitment firm.

The greatest time commitment for the recruitment committee members will of course be required when the facility plans and implements its own program. The discussion of the roles of recruitment committee members in the present section applies to this program option. If the planning committee decides to subcontract the planning of the development stages to an outside recruiting firm and have the hospital implement the program itself, the recruitment committee members will have implementation responsibilities of the program. If it is decided to have the hospital do the planning and development of the program itself and to subcontract for the implementation stages, the planning committee will have the major responsibility in the development process. In this case, the recruitment committee will have little interaction with the outside recruitment firm during the implementation of the program, except for the provision of assistance during physician area visits. If the hospital decides to subcontract the entire program to an outside firm, the recruitment committee will have little involvement in the total process, again except for providing some assistance during the physician visits.

MEMBER ROLE DESCRIPTIONS

In general, the members of the recruitment committee will be actively engaged in the search for sources, in the preinterview process, in the interview, in the follow-up, and in the retention of the recruited physician. The following role descriptions identify those members of the committee who will be actively involved in the hospital's recruitment effort: the administrator, the governing board member, the medical staff member, and community leaders.

Administrator

The hospital administrator is the leader in the recruitment process. As the committee chair, the administrator has the job of coordinating all efforts of the committee. As we have noted, a large time commitment is necessary for the recruitment effort, and it is important that the administrator dedicate the necessary time for this purpose. A recent trend in many hospitals is to designate a staff member as a medical staff representative and/or liaison or director of professional relations. If available, this staff member can play an important role in assisting the hospital administrator.

The administrator has the following responsibilities in the recruitment effort:

- The administrator should identify the other individuals who will form the recruitment committee and also the other responsible people who desire to be active in the recruitment process.
- The administrator should coordinate the flow of information to the various individuals involved in the recruitment process and serve as the liaison between the governing board, medical staff, community leaders, and potential candidates.
- The administrator should identify the people who are able to assist in locating physician sources.
- The administrator should determine who is responsible for developing the marketing brochures for the hospital. These brochures should utilize the information developed from the market analysis.
- The administrator and other committee members should coordinate efforts in the interviewing stage. The administrator will normally have the responsibility of prescreening the physician candidate, arranging for the physician and his family's site visit, and reviewing the physician's credentials.
- The administrator should have a key role in the follow-up. The administrator has an important responsibility in maintaining an ongoing relationship with the physician candidate until the final decision is made.
- The administrator should be concerned with the retention of the recruited physician. This should involve the administrator during the entire time that the recruited physician resides in the community.

Governing Board Member

The governing board member on the recruitment committee, may be the governing board representative on the planning committee. This member's responsibilities will be specified by the administrator, the head of the recruitment committee. The governing board member should become actively involved as a resource person throughout the recruitment process, assuming the following responsibilities:

- The governing board member should, if possible, provide contacts for the physician with regard to housing, the physician's career, schooling, and other relevant areas.
- If the governing board member is female, she might be able to befriend the physician's wife, invite her to lunch, and take her on a tour of the community. In this connection, it is the committee's responsibility to determine the specific interests of the spouse and how the community can best accommodate them.

- If the governing board member is involved in banking in the community, the member may be able to provide loan information and assist in obtaining financing for the new physician.
- If it has been decided to utilize an outside recruitment firm, the governing board member can assume a very active role with the firm, serving as liaison between the firm and the hospital.

Medical Staff Members

It is extremely important to select as committee members physicians who share the view that additional physicians are needed in the community. Medical staff interest and support are not necessarily automatic; they must be cultivated and nurtured on an ongoing basis. Some of the existing physicians may be antagonistic to a newly recruited physician, causing problems and negative feelings among the hospital's medical staff.

The physicians who are selected as committee members will play an important role in presenting the medical side of the practice situation. How does the hospital treat its physicians? What kind of referral patterns can the incoming physician expect? Who are the most influential and successful staff members and admitters? What is the patient population? (These questions will be dealt with in detail in the following chapters.)

The medical staff member of the recruitment committee has the following responsibilities:

- The medical staff member will be actively involved in most aspects of the recruitment effort. This member can assist in the need analysis by offering expert guidance in evaluating the statistical data. Many times, the data alone will not present a complete picture of the medical community. Medical staff input at this stage will thus be very beneficial.
- The medical staff member can assist in the development of the financial package for the recruited physician. This input can be valuable in determining costs and necessities in starting a medical practice.
- During the process of locating physician sources, the medical staff member can be involved in contacting colleagues in the community, medical schools, and residency programs. These can be excellent sources of physicians wishing to relocate or of young residents searching for practice opportunities.
- During the interviewing process, the medical staff member should be involved in meetings with the physician candidate, discussing the hospital and medical staff environment, referral patterns, patient flow, medical staff availability, and continuing medical education.

- During the follow-up stage, the medical staff member can contact the prospective physician candidate and emphasize how interested the medical community is in having him relocate to the area.
- The medical staff member should also be involved in the retention phase, encouraging other physicians to refer to the new staff member, inviting him to social events, and facilitating his exposure to other physicians in the area. In this way, the recruited physician will feel welcome and become fully integrated into the general medical community.

Community Members

It is important to choose as committee members representatives of the community who are dedicated to the recruitment process. Community leaders who would like to be actively involved in the hospital's efforts should be identified. Meetings with these leaders should be held to discuss the various needs and issues. The primary purpose would be to organize the community's support. Community participation in the recruitment process will help to create a positive feeling when the physician and his family visit the community.

Areas of responsibility should be assigned to the community representatives by the administrator. Dividing the work among various community members will make the recruitment process more efficient and generate a broader support base.

The following responsibilities of the community members of the recruitment committee are similar to those of the governing board member.

- The women from the community on the recruitment committee can serve in many ways. They can befriend the physician's wife and escort her to reception parties, luncheons, and afternoon teas and provide guided tours. For these functions, people should be invited who will be congenial and make the physician's wife feel at ease.
- If the community member is a banker or financial leader, the member can aid in presenting financial opportunities to the physician.
- A community member who is involved with real estate might discuss housing opportunities with the physician and his wife. In this regard, the financial situation of the prospective physician should not be automatically assumed. In showing houses to the physician, it is important to include various price ranges and not to concentrate only on the most expensive areas of town.
- If the physician has children, the community member can enlist the aid of people who are knowledgeable of the area's educational system.

SUMMARY

The above-mentioned committee members—the administrator and representatives of the governing board, the medical staff, and the community—will have the ultimate responsibility for the success of the physician recruitment program.

Chapter 8

Physician Sources

There are many physician resources that a hospital should review when implementing a physician recruitment program. The head of the recruitment committee should appoint the individual committee members who will actively pursue physician sources. These sources include residency programs and medical schools, professional journals, medical conferences, licensing boards, osteopathic physicians, referrals from community physicians, and foreign medical graduates.

RESIDENCY PROGRAMS AND MEDICAL SCHOOLS

Residency programs are excellent resource tools for finding and recruiting a physician. A physician in the final years of training will begin researching potential practice opportunities. Some residents postpone their final decision until their last year of the program, but most begin seeking available opportunities in their second or third year of residency.

The first step in utilizing this source is to locate the programs in the area. Then, the residents who are specializing in the medical discipline that the area requires should be contacted. A geographical listing of medical schools is presented in Appendix 8–A. Using this list, the recruitment committee can target the schools closest to its area and focus on their corresponding residency programs. The most recent AMA *Directory of Residency Training Programs* can be used as a guide in contacting specific residencies, the chiefs of service, and program directors.[1]

The recruitment committee should focus on the residents graduating in June who have not already committed themselves to a specific practice situation. If the residents that are contacted are already committed, the recruitment committee should still send them information on the practice opportunity, since they may have interested friends or can keep the information as a reference in case a committed position falls through. If the contacted resident is not committed, an informative brochure should be sent out immediately under a cover letter, detailing the opportunities available in the community.

A follow-up phone call within one week is critical to ensure continuity with the physician candidate. The physician should be encouraged to make a visit to the community and hospital. The committee should impress on the physician the critical need for a new physician and should stress the great opportunities available in the community. The committee should arrange a phone call from a local physician to welcome the incoming physician.

It is important that contact with the resident be maintained, since interest in the practice opportunity might well grow stronger as the graduation date approaches. Information brochures and letters should be sent to the medical directors of the programs, and personal follow-up phone calls should be made, detailing the situation.

Residency programs outside the immediate area should be contacted, using the same approach to reach the residents. If any of the residency programs that are contacted have a newsletter, advertisements describing the practice opportunity should be placed in it.

PROFESSIONAL JOURNALS

The placement of advertisements in journals and other physician-related publications is an effective recruitment technique. The specialty journal corresponding to the specialty of the physician the hospital is seeking is an excellent source in which to place the advertisement. A list of sample journals that offer classified advertisements is presented in Appendix 8-B.

Other sources are state medical societies and associations that publish magazines or bulletins that advertise potential practice opportunities and available physicians. A list of such societies and associations is provided in Appendix 8-C. Professional associations and societies may also publish periodicals or bulletins that list potential opportunities and available physicians. A list of such organizations that can be contacted for possible physician recruits is presented in Appendix 8-D.

Advertisements can also be placed in the general media, such as newspapers or leisure magazines, or in any reading material that a physician might be exposed to. The advertisements should be large and attractive yet concise, and they should describe the important characteristics of the practice opportunity and setting. Most journals have a lengthy time span between the request for the advertisement and its subsequent publication. The recruitment committee should keep this factor in mind when sending in the advertisement request.

MEDICAL MEETINGS AND LICENSING BOARDS

Conferences

Local or national conferences of physicians provide opportunities to meet with a large number of physicians in a short period of time. In such a meeting of a given specialty, there are likely to be physicians looking for new practice situations. Such meetings and conferences provide hospital representatives the opportunity to discuss the practice situation that is being offered and to distribute pertinent information.

The list of upcoming medical meetings should be periodically reviewed to see which ones will provide the best opportunities to market the particular practice situation. Current listings of medical meetings and conferences may be obtained by writing *Medical Meetings,* the international guide for health care meeting planners, published by United Business Publications, 475 Park Avenue South, New York, N.Y. 10016.

Licensing Boards

Before a new physician can set up a practice in an area, a state license must be obtained. Each state has its own particular licensing policies and procedures (see Appendix 8–E). Committee members should discover when the licensing board tests the physician candidates and, if a meeting is held, try to attend. This can provide one more way by which incoming physicians can be notified of potential practice opportunities.

OTHER PHYSICIANS

Osteopathic Physicians

Osteopathic physicians are a good source for physician candidates. Doctors of osteopathic medicine (D.O.'s) are fully trained and licensed physicians who practice in all 50 states. They are qualified to perform surgery and to prescribe medicine, and they have the same medical practice rights and professional obligations as M.D.'s, as established by state and national laws.[2]

More than 70 percent of osteopathic physicians are general practitioners, although many are also certified for practice in the medical specialties. D.O.'s make up five percent of the total physicians in the United States, yet they treat ten percent of the patients.

Osteopathic medicine places special emphasis on the musculoskeletal system. A special method, osteomanipulative therapy, is used for diagnosing and treating disorders of the musculoskeletal system. This method, used alone or with surgery and prescription medicines, provides the osteopathic physician and surgeon a unique dimension in the diagnosis and treatment of illness.

D.O. medical students receive all the training M.D. students do. In addition, they receive 300 to 500 hours of training throughout their medical schooling in osteopathic principles concerning the interrelationship of body systems in health and disease. They also receive special teaching in osteopathic palpatory diagnosis and manipulative therapy.

Community Physicians

Another excellent source for physicians is the existing medical community. The physicians in the area may know of a physician who is interested in relocating.

Thus, the practice opportunity should be discussed with members of the medical staff to see if they know of any interested individuals and if they will assist in the hospital's recruitment efforts. Through their contacts with other physicians, medical staff members can disseminate information regarding the practice opportunity.

FOREIGN MEDICAL GRADUATES

A foreign medical graduate (FMG) is a physician who is trained outside the United States.[3] This includes physicians trained in any foreign country including Canada and Mexico.

Although Canadian-trained physicians are considered foreign medical graduates because they are trained outside the United States, due to similar training styles in the two countries, many states have reciprocal licensing arrangements with Canada for these physicians. Those states without reciprocal procedures require specific examinations that vary from state to state.

The one drawback in recruiting Canadian physicians is in the problem of immigration. In some instances, it takes as long as 18 months to process all of the immigration papers necessary for a Canadian physician to move to the United States. If the recruitment committee wishes to utilize a Canadian physician as a resource, it should be aware of the time problem involved in the recruiting process.

The following data summarize the way in which FMGs are distributed at the national and state level:

- FMGs constitute approximately one-third of all interns and residents in the United States.
- Approximately one-half of all FMGs are located in only five states.

• Only 7 percent of active FMGs practice in nonmetropolitan areas, where the most critical shortages of physician services exist, compared with 14 percent of United States medical graduates.

• FMGs gravitate toward the highly urbanized centers of the country to an even greater extent than do United States medical graduates.[4]

Since foreign-trained physicians are a reality and their numbers are steadily increasing, it behooves the committee to examine their viability in the community. Will the community accept and support the new foreign-trained physician? Are there built-in prejudices that will have to be overcome prior to such a physician beginning practice? Will the medical staff welcome and lend its support to such a physician, both socially and medically? If the committee gives the green light, the procedure necessary for foreign medical graduates licensure should be instituted. The relevant medical licensure requirements are contained in Appendix 8–F.

NOTES

1. American Medical Association, *Directory of Residency Training Programs, 1980–1981* (Monroe, Wis.: American Medical Association, 1980), pp. 483–488.

2. Matt Weyuker, *The Complete Physician* (Sacramento: Osteopathic Physicians and Surgeons of California, 1980), p. 2.

3. Educational Commission for Foreign Medical Graduates (ECFMG), *Handbook for Foreign Medical Graduates,* (Philadelphia: ECFMG, 1976), p. 4.

4. Beverly C. Martin, "Urban/Rural Distribution of Foreign Medical Graduates," in *Socioeconomic Issues of Health, 1975–1976,* ed. Henry R. Mason (Chicago: American Medical Association, 1976), p. 62.

Appendix 8–A

Geographical Listing of Medical Schools

UNITED STATES

Alabama
University of Alabama School of Medicine
University of South Alabama College of Medicine

Arizona
University of Arizona College of Medicine

Arkansas
University of Arkansas College of Medicine

California
University of California, Davis, School of Medicine
University of California, Irvine, School of Medicine
University of California, Los Angeles, School of Medicine
University of California, San Diego, School of Medicine
University of California, San Francisco, School of Medicine
Charles R. Drew Postgraduate Medical School
Loma Linda University School of Medicine
University of Southern California School of Medicine
Stanford University School of Medicine

Colorado
University of Colorado School of Medicine

Connecticut
University of Connecticut School of Medicine
Yale University School of Medicine

District of Columbia
Georgetown University School of Medicine
George Washington University

Source: Reprinted from the *Directory of American Medical Education, 1978–1979* of the Association of American Medical Colleges, pp. vi–ix. Used by permission.

School of Medicine and
Health Sciences
Howard University College of
Medicine

Florida
University of Florida College
of Medicine (including
FSU-FAMU program)
University of Miami School of
Medicine
University of South Florida
College of Medicine

Georgia
Emory University School of
Medicine
Medical College of Georgia
School of Medicine
School of Medicine at
Morehouse College

Hawaii
University of Hawaii John A.
Burns School of Medicine

Illinois
University of Chicago/The
Pritzker School of Medicine
University of Health
Sciences/The
Chicago Medical School
University of Illinois College of
Medicine
Loyola University of Chicago
Stritch School of Medicine
Northwestern University
Medical School
Rush Medical College
Southern Illinois University
School of Medicine

Indiana
Indiana University School of
Medicine

Iowa
University of Iowa College of
Medicine

Kansas
University of Kansas School
of Medicine

Kentucky
University of Kentucky College
of Medicine
University of Louisville
School of Medicine

Louisiana
Louisiana State University
School of Medicine in New
Orleans
Louisiana State University
School of Medicine
in Shreveport
Tulane University School of
Medicine

Maryland
Johns Hopkins University
School of Medicine
University of Maryland School
of Medicine
Uniformed Services University
of the Health Sciences
School of Medicine

Massachusetts
Boston University School of
Medicine
Harvard Medical School
University of Massachusetts
Medical School
Tufts University School of
Medicine

Michigan
Michigan State University
College of Human Medicine

University of Michigan
Medical School
Wayne State University School
of Medicine

Minnesota
Mayo Medical School
University of Minnesota -
Duluth School of Medicine
University of Minnesota
Medical School -
Minneapolis

Mississippi
University of Mississippi
School of Medicine

Missouri
University of Missouri -
Columbia School of
Medicine
University of Missouri -
Kansas City School of
Medicine
Saint Louis University School
of Medicine
Washington University School
of Medicine

Nebraska
Creighton University School
of Medicine
University of Nebraska
College of Medicine

Nevada
University of Nevada School
of Medical Science

New Hampshire
Dartmouth Medical School

New Jersey
College of Medicine and
Dentistry of New Jersey/
New Jersey Medical School

College of Medicine and
Dentistry of New Jersey
Rutgers Medical School

New Mexico
University of New Mexico
School of Medicine

New York
Albany Medical College of
Union University
Albert Einstein College of
Medicine of Yeshiva
University
Columbia University College
of Physicians and Surgeons
Cornell University Medical
College
Mount Sinai School of
Medicine of the City
University of New York
New York Medical College
New York University School
of Medicine
University of Rochester School
of Medicine and Dentistry
State University of New York
at Buffalo School of
Medicine
State University of New York
Downstate Medical Center
College of Medicine
State University of New York
at Stony Brook Health
Sciences Center
School of Medicine
State University of New York
Upstate Medical Center
College of Medicine

North Carolina
Bowman Gray School of
Medicine of Wake Forest
University

Duke University School of
Medicine
East Carolina University
School of Medicine
University of North Carolina
School of Medicine

North Dakota
University of North Dakota
School of Medicine

Ohio
Case Western Reserve
University School of
Medicine
University of Cincinnati
College of Medicine
Medical College of Ohio at
Toledo
Northeastern Ohio Universities
College of Medicine
Ohio State University College
of Medicine
Wright State University
School of Medicine

Oklahoma
University of Oklahoma
College of Medicine

Oregon
University of Oregon School of
Medicine

Pennsylvania
Hahnemann Medical College
Jefferson Medical College of
Thomas Jefferson University
Medical College of
Pennsylvania
Pennsylvania State University
College of Medicine
University of Pennsylvania
School of Medicine
University of Pittsburgh

School of Medicine
Temple University School of
Medicine

Rhode Island
Brown University Program in
Medicine

South Carolina
Medical University of South
Carolina College of
Medicine
University of South Carolina
School of Medicine

South Dakota
University of South Dakota
School of Medicine

Tennessee
Meharry Medical College
School of Medicine
University of Tennessee
College of Medicine
Vanderbilt University School
of Medicine

Texas
Baylor College of Medicine
Texas A&M University
College of Medicine
Texas Tech University School
of Medicine
University of Texas
Southwestern
Medical School at Dallas
University of Texas Medical
School at Galveston
University of Texas Medical
School at Houston
University of Texas Medical
School at San Antonio

Utah
University of Utah College of
Medicine

Vermont
University of Vermont College
of Medicine

Virginia
Eastern Virginia Medical
School
University of Virginia School
of Medicine
Virginia Commonwealth
University Medical College
of Virginia School
of Medicine

Washington
University of Washington
School of Medicine

West Virginia
Marshall University School of
Medicine
West Virginia University
School of Medicine

Wisconsin
Medical College of Wisconsin
University of Wisconsin
Medical School

PUERTO RICO

Catholic University of Puerto
Rico School of Medicine
University of Puerto Rico
School of Medicine

BEIRUT, LEBANON

American University of Beirut
School of Medicine

CANADA

Alberta
University of Alberta Faculty

of Medicine
University of Calgary Faculty
of Medicine

British Columbia
University of British Columbia
Faculty of Medicine

Manitoba
University of Manitoba
Medical Faculty

Newfoundland
Memorial University of
Newfoundland Faculty of
Medicine

Nova Scotia
Dalhousie University Faculty
of Medicine

Ontario
McMaster University
Faculty of Health Sciences
University of Ottawa
Faculty of Medicine
Queen's University
Faculty of Medicine
University of Toronto
Faculty of Medicine
University of Western Ontario
Faculty of Medicine

Quebec
Laval University
Faculty of Medicine
McGill University
Faculty of Medicine
University of Montreal
Faculty of Medicine
University of Sherbrooke
Faculty of Medicine

Saskatchewan
University of Saskatchewan
College of Medicine

Appendix 8-B

Professional Journals That Carry Classified Advertisements

American Family Physician
Box 1510
3075 Saturn
Clearwater, Fla. 33517

*American Journal of Obstetrics
  and Gynecology*
John I. Brewer, Editor-in-Chief
303 E. Superior Street, Room 1018
Chicago, Ill. 60611
(312) 266-5266

The D.O.
212 E. Ohio Street
Chicago, Ill. 60611

Emergency Medicine
Irving J. Cohen, Editor
280 Madison Avenue
New York, N.Y. 10016
(212) 889-4530

Hospital & Community Psychiatry
Editor
1700 18th Street, N.W.
Washington, D.C. 20009
(202) 797-4918

Hospital Physician
F & F Publications, Inc.
515 Madison Avenue
New York, N.Y. 10022

Hospitals
American Hospital Publishing Inc.
211 E. Chicago Ave.
Chicago, Ill. 60611
(312) 951-1100

*Journal of the American Medical
  Association*
Classified Advertising Department
535 N. Dearborn St.
Chicago, Ill. 60610

*Journal of the American
  Osteopathic Association*
212 East Ohio Street
Chicago, Ill. 60611
(312) 280-5800

Journal of Family Practice
John P. Geyman, Editor
Professor and Chairman,
    Department of Family Medicine

Source: Reprinted from the list of sample journals compiled by Medical Career Services.

RF 30, School of Medicine,
    University of Washington
Seattle, Wash. 98195
(206) 543–1060

*Journal of the National Medical
    Association*
Calvin Sampson, Editor
Editorial Office
1720 Massachusetts Ave., N.W.
Washington, D.C. 20036
(202) 659–9623 or 636–6306

Medical Economics
680 Kinderkamack Road
Oradell, N.J. 07649
(201) 262–3030

Medical World News
1221 Avenue of the Americas
New York, N.Y. 10020

Military Medicine
P.O. Box 104
10605 Concord St., Suite 306
Kensington, Md. 20795

New England Journal of Medicine
10 Shattuck Street
Boston, Mass. 02115

New Physicians
P.O. Box 131
14650 Lee Road
Chantilly, Va. 22021

Pediatrics
Jerold F. Lucey

Editorial Office
Mary Fletcher Hospital
Colchester Avenue
Burlington, Vt. 05401
(802) 869–4244

Physician and Sports Medicine
Editorial Department
4530 West 77th Street
Minneapolis, Minn. 55435

Postgraduate Medicine
Editorial Department
4530 West 77th Street
Minneapolis, Minn. 55435
(612) 835–3222

Psychiatric News
1700 18th Street, N.W.
Washington, D.C. 20009
(202) 797–4918

Resident & Staff Physician
80 Shore Road
Port Washington, N.Y. 11050
(516) 883–6350

Rocky Mountain Medical Journal
1601 East 19th Avenue
Denver, Colo. 80218
(303) 861–1221

Texas Medicine
1905 N. Lamar Blvd.
Austin, Tex. 78705
(512) 477–6704

Appendix 8–C

State Medical Societies and Associations

Medical Association of the
State of Alabama
19 South Jackson Street
Montgomery, Ala. 36104

Alaska State Medical Association
1135 West 8th Ave. #6
Anchorage, Alaska 99501

Arizona Medical Association
810 West Bethany Home Road
Phoenix, Ariz. 85013

Arkansas Medical Society
P. O. Box 1208
Fort Smith, Ark. 72901

California Medical Association
731 Market St.
San Francisco, Calif. 94105

Colorado Medical Association
1601 East 19th Avenue
Denver, Colo. 80218

Connecticut State Medical
Association

160 St. Ronan St.
New Haven, Conn. 06511

Medical Society of Delaware
1925 Lovering Ave.
Wilmington, Del. 19806

Medical Society of the
District of Columbia
2007 Eye St., N.W.
Washington, D.C. 20006

Florida Medical Association
P. O. Box 2411
Jacksonville, Fla. 32203

Medical Association of Georgia
938 Peachtree St., N.E.
Atlanta, Ga. 30309

Guam Medical Society
P. O. Box 8198
Tamuning, Guam 96911

Hawaii Medical Association
320 Ward Ave. #200
Honolulu, Hawaii 96814

Source: Reprinted from the reference directories of the State Medical Associations, *Journal of the American Medical Association,* 244, no. 21 (©1980): 2401–2404. Used by permission.

Idaho Medical Association
P. O. Box 2668
Boise, Idaho 83701

Illinois State Medical Society
55 E. Monroe, Suite 3510
Chicago, Ill. 60603

Indiana State Medical
Association
3935 N. Meridian St.
Indianapolis, Ind. 46208

Iowa Medical Society
1001 Grand Ave.
West Des Moines, Iowa 50265

Medical Association of the
Isthmian Canal Zone
Box M
Balboa Heights, C.Z. 00101

Kansas Medical Society
1300 Topeka Ave.
Topeka, Kans. 66612

Kentucky Medical Association
3532 Ephraim McDowell Dr.
Louisville, Ky. 40205

Louisiana State Medical Society
1700 Josephine St.
New Orleans, La. 70113

Maine Medical Association
524 Western Ave.
Augusta, Maine 04330

Medical and Chirurgical Faculty
of the State of Maryland
1211 Cathedral Street
Baltimore, Md. 21201

Massachusetts Medical Society
22 The Fenway
Boston, Mass. 02215

Michigan State Medical Society

120 W. Saginaw St.
East Lansing, Mich. 48823

Minnesota State Medical
Association
American National Bank Bldg.
#900
St. Paul, Minn. 55101

Mississippi State Medical
Association
735 Riverside Dr.
Jackson, Miss. 39216

Missouri State Medical Association
P. O. Box 1028
Jefferson City, Mo. 65102

Montana Medical Association
2021 11th Ave., Suite 12
Helena, Mont. 59601

Nebraska Medical Association
1512 1st National Bank Bldg.
Lincoln, Nebr. 68501

Nevada State Medical Association
3660 Baker Lane
Reno, Nev. 89502

New Hampshire Medical Society
4 Park Street
Concord, N.H. 03301

Medical Society of New Jersey
2 Princess Road
Lawrence, N.J. 08648

New Mexico Medical Society
2650 Yale Blvd., S.E.
Albuquerque, N. Mex. 87106

Medical Society of the State
of New York
420 Lakeville Road
Lake Success, N.Y. 11042

North Carolina Medical Society

P. O. Box 27167
Raleigh, N.C. 27611

North Dakota Medical Association
P. O. Box 1198
Bismarck, N. Dak. 58501

Ohio State Medical Association
600 South High Street
Columbus, Ohio 43215

Oklahoma State Medical
    Association
601 N.W. Expressway
Oklahoma City, Okla. 73118

Oregon Medical Association
5210 S.W. Corbett
Portland, Oreg. 97201

Pennsylvania Medical Society
20 Erford Road
Lemoyne, Pa. 10743

Puerto Rico Medical Association
P. O. Box 9387
Santurce, P.R. 00908

Rhode Island Medical Society
106 Francis Street
Providence, R.I. 02903

South Carolina Medical
    Association
3325 Medical Park Road
Columbus, S.C. 29203

South Dakota State Medical
    Association
Sioux Falls, S. Dak. 57104

Tennessee Medical Association
112 Louise Ave.
Nashville, Tenn. 37203

Texas Medical Association
1801 N. Lamar Blvd.
Austin, Tex. 78701

U.S. Virgin Island Medical Society
Box 9626
St. Thomas, V.I. 00801

Utah State Medical Association
540 E. Fifth St.
Salt Lake City, Utah 84102

Vermont State Medical Society
136 Main St.
Montpelier, Vt. 05602

Medical Society of Virginia
4205 Dover Road
Richmond, Va. 23221

Washington State Medical
    Association
2033 Sixth Ave. #900
Seattle, Wash. 98121

West Virginia State Medical
    Association
P. O. Box 1031
Charleston, W. Va. 25324

State Medical Society of Wisconsin
Box 1109
Madison, Wis. 53701

Wyoming State Medical Society
P. O. Box 4009
Cheyenne, Wyo. 82001

Appendix 8–D

Professional Organizations

American Academy of
Dermatology, Inc.
Bradford W. Claxton, Exec.
Director
820 Davis St.
Evanston, Ill. 60201
(312) 869–3954

American Academy of Facial
Plastic and Reconstructive
Surgery, Inc.
Thomas Nelson, Exec. Dir.
70 W. Hubbard #202
Chicago, Ill. 60610
(312) 644–2623

American Academy of Family
Physicians
Roger Tusken, Exec. Director
1740 W. 92nd St.
Kansas City, Mo. 64114
(816) 333–9700

American Academy of Neurology
Stanley A. Nelson, Exec. Dir.
4015 W. 65th St., Suite 302

Minneapolis, Minn. 55435
(612) 920–3636

American Academy of
Ophthalmology
Bruce Spivey, Exec. Dir.
1833 Filmore
San Francisco, Calif. 94120
(415) 563–5725

American Academy of Orthopaedic
Surgeons
Charles V. Heck, Exec. Dir.
444 N. Michigan Ave.
Chicago, Ill. 60611
(312) 822–0970

American Academy of
Otolaryngology
Wesley H. Bradley, Exec. V.P.
15 2nd St., S.W.
Rochester, Minn. 55901
(507) 288–7444

American Academy of Pediatrics
Robert G. Frazier, Exec. Dir.

Source: Reprinted with permission, from *American Hospital Association Guide to the Health Care Field,* published by the American Hospital Association, © 1980, pp. C3–C11.

1801 Hinman Ave.
Evanston, Ill. 60204
(312) 869-4255

American Academy of Physical
  Medicine and Rehabilitation
Creston C. Herold, Exec. Dir.
30 N. Michigan Ave., Suite 922
Chicago, Ill. 60602
(312) 236-9512

American Association for the
  Surgery of Trauma
George Sheldon, Sec., Dept. of
  Surgery
San Francisco General Hospital
1001 Potrero
San Francisco, Calif. 94110
(415) 821-8814

American Association of
  Obstetricians and Gynecologists
Edgar L. Makowski, Sec.
4200 E. 9th Ave.
Denver, Colo. 80262
(303) 394-7616

American Association of
  Ophthalmology
Lawrence A. Zupan, Exec. Sec.
1100 17th Street, N.W., Suite 901
Washington, D.C. 20036
(202) 833-3447

American Association of
  Pathologists
Kenneth Endicott, Exec. Off.
9651 Rockville Pike
Bethesda, Md. 20014
(301) 530-7130

American Association of Plastic
  Surgeons
F. E. Bennett, Sec.
236 Emerson Hall

1100 W. Michigan
Indianapolis, Ind. 46223
(317) 264-8106

American College of Cardiology
William D. Nelligan, Exec. Dir.
9111 Old Georgetown Road
Bethesda, Md. 20014
(301) 897-5400

American College of Chest
  Physicians
Alfred Soffer, Exec. Dir.
911 Busse Hwy.
Park Ridge, Ill. 60068
(312) 698-2200

American College of Emergency
  Physicians
Arthur E. Auer, Exec. Dir.
3900 Capital City Blvd.
Lansing, Mich. 48906
(517) 321-7911

American College of
  Gastroenterology
Daniel Weiss, Exec. Dir.
299 Broadway
New York, N.Y. 10007
(212) 227-7590

American College of Obstetricians
  and Gynecologists
Warren E. Pearse, Exec. Dir.
1 E. Wacker Dr.
Chicago, Ill. 60601
(312) 222-1600

American College of Physicians
Robert H. Moser, Exec. Vice Pres.
4200 Pine St.
Philadelphia, Pa. 19104
(215) 243-1200

American College of Radiology
William C. Stronach, Exec. Dir.

20 N. Wacker Dr., Room 2920
Chicago, Ill. 60606
(312) 236-4963

American College of Surgeons
C. Rollins Hanlon, Dir.
55 E. Erie St.
Chicago, Ill. 60611
(312) 664-4050

American Gynecological Society
Brian Little, Sec.
2065 Adelbert Rd.
Cleveland, Ohio 44106
(216) 444-3334

American Hospital Association
John Alexander McMahon, Pres.
840 N. Lake Shore Dr.
Chicago, Ill. 60611
(312) 280-6000

American Medical Association
James H. Sammons, Exec. Vice
  Pres.
535 N. Dearborn St.
Chicago, Ill. 60610
(312) 751-6000

American Medical Women's
  Association, Inc.
Lorraine Loesel, Exec. Dir.
1740 Broadway
New York, N.Y. 10019
(212) 586-8683

American Neurological Association
James Toole, Sec. Treas.
Bowman Gray School of Medicine
Box 29A
Dept. of Neurology
Winston-Salem, N.C. 27103
(919) 727-4598

American Orthopaedic Association
Lois Stratemeier, Exec. Sec.

444 N. Michigan Ave.
Chicago, Ill. 60611
(312) 822-0970

American Osteopathic Association
Edward P. Crowell, Exec. Dir.
212 E. Ohio St.
Chicago, Ill. 60611
(312) 944-2713

American Osteopathic Hospital
  Association
Michael F. Doody, Pres.
930 Busse Hwy.
Park Ridge, Ill. 60068
(312) 692-2351

American Pediatric Society, Inc.
David Goldring, Sec. Treas.
500 S. Kings Hwy.
St. Louis, Mo. 63110
(314) 367-6880

American Psychiatric Association
Melvin Sabshin, Med. Dir.
1700 18th St., N.W.
Washington, D.C. 20009
(202) 797-4882

American Society for Head and
  Neck Surgery
Jerome C. Goldstein, Sec.
Division of Otolaryngology
Albany Medical College
Albany, N.Y. 12208
(518) 445-5575

American Society of
  Anesthesiologists
John W. Andes, Exec. Sec.
515 Busse Hwy.
Park Ridge, Ill. 60068
(312) 825-5586

American Society of Clinical
  Pathologists

(Includes Board of Registry)
Margaret A. McCormick, Dir.
P. O. Box 12270
Chicago, Ill. 60612
David L. Gilcrest, Exec. Dir.
2100 W. Harrison St.
Chicago, Ill. 60612
(312) 738-1336

American Society of Colon and
Rectal Surgeons
Harriette Gibson, Adm. Sec.
615 Griswold, Suite 516
Detroit, Mich. 48226
(313) 961-7880

American Society of Internal
Medicine
William R. Ramsey, Exec. V.P.
2550 M St. N.W., Suite 620
Washington, D.C. 20037
(202) 659-0330

American Society of
Ophthalmologic and
Otolaryngologic Allergy
William P. King, Sec. Treas.
1415 Third St., Suite 507
Corpus Christi, Tex. 78404
(512) 882-9228

American Society of Plastic and
Reconstructive Surgeons, Inc.
Dallas F. Whaley, Exec. V.P.
29 E. Madison St., Suite 800
Chicago, Ill. 60602
(312) 641-0593

American Surgical Association
James V. Maloney Jr., Sec.
UCLA Medical Center
Los Angeles, Calif. 90024
(213) 825-7017

American Thoracic Society

S.R. Iannotta, Exec. Dir.
1740 Broadway
New York, N.Y. 10019
(212) 245-8000

American Urological Association,
Inc.
Richard J. Hannigan, Exec. Sec.
1120 N. Charles St.
Baltimore, Md. 21201
(301) 727-1100

Association of American Physicians
Charles C. J. Carpenter, Sec.
University Hospitals
Cleveland, Ohio 44106
(216) 444-3245

Association of American Physicians
and Surgeons, Inc.
Frank K. Woolley, Exec. Dir.
8991 Cotswold Dr.
Burke, Va. 22015
(703) 425-6300

Central Association of
Obstetricians and Gynecologists
Davis G. Anderson, Sec. Treas.
Women's Hospital
University of Michigan Medical
Center
Ann Arbor, Mich. 48109
(313) 763-2033

Committee of Interns and
Residents
Edward T. Gluckmann, Exec. Dir.
386 Park Ave. S
New York, N.Y. 10016
(212) 725-5500

Council of Medical Specialty
Societies
Richard S. Wilbur, Exec. V.P.
Box 70

Lake Forest, Ill. 60045
(312) 295-3456

National Federation of Catholic
  Physicians Guilds
Robert H. Herzog, Exec. Sec.
850 Elm Grove Rd.
Elm Grove, Wis. 53122
(414) 784-3435

National Medical Association, Inc.
Alfred F. Fisher, Exec. Dir.
1720 Massachusetts Ave. N.W.
Washington, D.C. 20036
(202) 659-9623

National Resident Matching
  Program
John S. Graettinger, Exec. V.P.

1603 Orrington Ave., Suite 1155
Evanston, Ill. 60201
(312) 328-3440

Neurosurgical Society of America
James Story, Sec.
University of Texas Health Science
  Center, Division of Neurosurgery
7703 Floyd Curl Dr.
San Antonio, Tex. 78284
(512) 691-6136

Physicians Service Association
Marvin D. Kline, Pres.
6303 Barfield Rd. N.E.
Atlanta, Ga. 30328
(404) 394-7700, outside Ga. (800)
  241-6905

Appendix 8-E

State Examinations and Licensure

Educational Commission for Foreign Medical Graduates (ECFMG). Exec Dir: R. L. Casterline, 3624 Market St, Philadelphia, Pa. 19104.

National Board of Medical Examiners. Pres: E. J. Levit, 3930 Chestnut St., Philadelphia, Pa. 19104.

Basic Science Board

Arkansas. Examination: April and October. Sec: A. W. Ford, State Department of Education, Education Building, Little Rock, Ark. 72201.

District of Columbia. Examination: May and November. Reciprocity: April and October. Chief: D. Krause, Commission on Licensure, 614 H St NW, Washington, D.C. 20001.

South Dakota. Examination: January, June, and November.

Reciprocity or Waiver: Continuous. Clerk: D. Willadsen, Law Building, Parker, S. Dak. 57053.

Utah. Examination: Quarterly. Reciprocity: Some. Info: R. E. Casper, Director, Department of Registration, 330 E Fourth St., Salt Lake City, Utah 84111.

Washington. Examination: Semiannually. Reciprocity: Six times per year. Exec Sec: J. Redmond, Division of Professional Licensing, Box 9649, Olympia, Wash. 98501.

Boards of Medical Examiners

(States marked by asterisks [*] require a basic science certificate.)

Alabama. Examination: FLEX. Montgomery. Exec Sec: R. Parker, PO Box 946, Montgomery, Ala. 36102.

Alaska. Examination: FLEX. Anchorage. Reciprocity:

Source: Reprinted from the reference directories for examinations and licensure, *Journal of the American Medical Association,* 244, no. 21 (©1980): 2405. Used by permission.

Continuous. Sec: Division of Occupational Licensing, Department of Commerce, Pouch "D", Juneau, Alaska 99801.

Arizona. Examination: FLEX. Oral Examination: Quarterly. Endorsement: Continuous Exec Dir: P. Boykin, 506 N 19th Ave, Third Floor West, Phoenix, Ariz. 85015.

Arkansas.* Examination: FLEX. Sec: J. Verser, Box 102, Harrisburg, Ark. 72432.

California. Examination: FLEX. Reciprocity: Weekly. Info: 1430 Howe Ave, Sacramento, Calif. 95825.

Canal Zone. Previous holders of a Canal Zone license may obtain information concerning their license from the Office of Health and Safety, Panama Canal Commission, APO, Miami, Fla. 34011.

Colorado. Examination: FLEX. Reciprocity: Quarterly. Exec Sec: L. W. Arduser, 1525 Sherman, Denver, Colo. 80203.

Connecticut.* Examination: FLEX. Hartford. Reciprocity: Continuous. Exec Dir: S. A. Harriman, 79 Elm St, Hartford, Conn. 06115.

Delaware. Examination: FLEX. M. J. Clark, Jesse S. Cooper Building, Dover, Del. 19901.

District of Columbia.* Examination: FLEX. Chief: D. Krause, Commission on Licensure, 614 H St NW, Washington, D.C. 20001.

Florida. Examination: FLEX. Exec Dir: D. J. Faircloth, 2009 Apalachee Pkwy, Tallahassee, Fla. 32301.

Georgia. Examination: FLEX. Sec: C. L. Clifton, 166 Pryor St SW, Atlanta, Ga. 30303.

Guam. Reciprocity: First Tuesday of each month. Sec: R. S. Sitkin, PO Box AX, Agana, Guam 96910.

Hawaii. Examination: FLEX. Sec: B. Tomasu, Dept of Regulatory Agencies, Box 541, Honolulu, Hawaii 96809.

Idaho. Examination: FLEX. Exec Dir: D. L. Deleski, PO Box 6817, 2621 W Idaho St, Boise, Idaho 83707.

Illinois. Examination: FLEX. Info: J. Anderson, 628 E Adams St, Springfield, Ill. 62786.

Indiana. Examination: FLEX. Reciprocity: Fourth Thursday each month. Sec: I. J. Kwitny, M & W Building, 700 N High School Rd, Indianapolis, Ind. 46224.

Iowa. Examination: FLEX. Exec Sec: R. V. Saf, 300 Fourth St., State Office Building, Des Moines, Iowa 50318.

Kansas. Examination: FLEX. Exec Sec: J. E. Hill, 503 Kansas Ave, Topeka, Kans. 66603.

Kentucky. Examination: FLEX. Endorsement and reciprocity: Continuous. Exec Sec: C. W. Schmidt, 3532 Ephraim McDowell Dr, Louisville, Ky. 40205.

Louisiana. Examination: FLEX. Sec: J. Morgan Lyons, 621 Hibernia Bank Bldg., New Orleans, La. 70112.

Maine. Examination: FLEX. Sec: G. E. Sullivan, 100 College Ave, Waterville, Maine 04901.

Maryland. Examination: FLEX. Sec: C. Bagley, 201 W Preston St, Baltimore, Md. 21201.

Massachusetts. Examination: FLEX. Sec: C. Cloutier, Room 1511, Leverett Saltonstall Bldg, 100 Cambridge, Boston, Mass. 02202.

Michigan. Examination: FLEX. Exec Dir: B. C. Brennan, PO Box 30018, 905 Southland, Lansing, Mich. 48909.

Minnesota. Examination: FLEX. Sec: A. Poore, 717 SE Delaware, Minneapolis, Minn. 55414.

Mississippi. Examination: FLEX. Sec: A. B. Cobb, Box 1700, Jackson, Miss. 39205.

Missouri. Examination: FLEX. Sec: G. Clark, Box 4, Jefferson City, Mo. 65101.

Montana. Examination: FLEX. Exec Sec: A. L. Goulding, Lalonde Bldg 4, Helena, Mont. 59601.

Nebraska. Examination: Omaha, FLEX. Reciprocity: When needed. Dir: R. C. Higley, State Office Building, 301 Centennial Mall S, Box 95007, Lincoln, Nebr. 68509.

Nevada. Examination: FLEX. Sec: J. Rogers, 1281 Terminal Way 211, Reno, Nev. 89502.

New Hampshire. Examination: FLEX. Exec Sec: M. H. Mires, 61 S Spring St, Concord, N.H. 03301.

New Jersey. Examination: FLEX. Exec Sec: A. J. Schuster, Board of Medical Examiners, 28 W State St, Trenton, N.J. 08625.

New Mexico. Examination: FLEX. Sec: R. C. Derbyshire, 210 E Marcy St, Santa Fe, N. Mex. 87501.

New York. Examination: FLEX. Endorsement: Continuous. Exec Sec: J. F. Roach, 99 Washington Ave, Albany, N.Y. 12230.

North Carolina. Examination: FLEX. Exec Sec: B. D. Paris Jr, 222 N Person St, Suite 214, Raleigh, N.C. 27601.

North Dakota. Examination: FLEX. Exec. Sec-Treas: L. A. Limond, Box 1198, Bismarck, N. Dak. 58501.

Ohio. Examination: FLEX. Admn: W. J. Lee, 65 S Front St, Suite 510, Columbus, Ohio 43215.

Oklahoma. Examination: FLEX. Exec Sec: B. J. Rogers, 3013 NW 59th St, Oklahoma City, Okla. 73112.

Oregon. Examination: FLEX. Exec Sec: G. Whelan, 1002 Loyalty Bldg., 317 SW Alder St, Portland, Oreg. 97204.

Pennsylvania. Examination: FLEX. Endorsement: Continuous. Sec: D. L. Bupp, 279 Boas St, Box 2649, Harrisburg, Pa. 17120.

Puerto Rico. Sec: M.D. Rodriquez, Box 3271, San Juan, P. R. 00904.

Rhode Island. Examination: FLEX. Admn: M.E. McCabe, Health Department Building, Davis Street, Providence, R.I. 02908.

South Carolina. Examination: FLEX. Exec Dir: N. B. Heyward, 1315 Blanding St, Columbia, S.C. 29201.

South Dakota.* Examination: FLEX. Exec Sec: R. D. Johnson, 608 West Ave N, Sioux Falls, S. Dak. 57104.

Tennessee. Examination: FLEX. Exec Sec: H. R. Foreman, Board of Medical Examiners, State Office Building, Ben Allen Road, Nashville, Tenn. 37216.

Texas.* Examination: FLEX. Sec: A. B. Spires, Jr, 211 E Seventh St, Suite 900, Austin, Tex. 78701.

Utah.* Examination: FLEX. Dir: P. T. Fordham, 330 E Fourth St, Salt Lake City, Utah 84111.

Vermont. Examination: FLEX. Endorsement: Continuous. Sec: E. S. Cross, Jr., Board of Medical Practice, 10 Baldwin St, Montpelier, Vt. 05602.

Virginia. Examination: FLEX. Exec Sec: F. J. Mayo, 3600 W. Broad St, Suite 453, Richmond, Va. 23230.

Virgin Islands. Sec: S. O. McDonald, PO Box 1442, St Thomas, V.I. 00801.

Washington.* Examination: FLEX. Exec Sec: J. Redmond, PO Box 9649, Olympia, Wash. 98504.

West Virginia. Examination: FLEX. Exec Sec: G. K. Pridemore, 1800 Washington St, Charleston, W. Va. 25305.

Wisconsin. Examination: FLEX. Sec: D. Zychowski, 1400 E Washington Ave, Madison, Wis. 53702.

Wyoming. Examination: FLEX. Exec Sec: L. J. Cohen, Hathaway Building, Cheyenne, Wyo. 82002.

Appendix 8–F

Medical Licensure Requirements

The information was provided by Lorna Wunderman of the staff of the AMA Center for Health Services Research and Development in cooperation with Arthur Osteen, Ph.D. of the Department of Physician Credentials and Qualification. The four tables are taken (with publication corrections) from "Physician Distribution and Medical Licensure in the U.S., 1979," published by the AMA.

POLICIES FOR INITIAL MEDICAL LICENSURE FOR GRADUATES OF U.S. MEDICAL SCHOOLS

The initial medical license of most U.S. medical school graduates is granted by endorsement of their National Board Certificates. All licensing jurisdictions, except Louisiana, Texas, and the Virgin Islands, will endorse certificates from the National Board. Texas will accept a National Board certificate earned prior to January 1, 1978, but not one earned after that date. Those graduates who are not licensed by endorsement of a National Board certificate, must pass the Federation Licensing Examination (FLEX) which is used by all states as their medical licensing examination. In many states the certificate of the National Board of Examiners for Osteopathic Physicians and Surgeons can be endorsed for licensure. Boards of medical examiners in Guam, Massachusetts, Oregon, Pennsylvania, Virginia, and West Virginia will endorse U.S. specialty board certificates for licensing purposes in specific circumstances as delineated by the licensure regulations of those states.

Source: Reprinted from "Medical Licensure Requirements," *Directory of Residency Training Programs, 1981–1982* (Chicago: American Medical Association, ©1981), pp. 483–488. Used by permission.

POLICIES FOR LICENSURE OF GRADUATES OF FOREIGN MEDICAL SCHOOLS

Most of the state medical boards will accept graduate training in Canada as equivalent to training undertaken in the U.S. Thirty-two states will issue a medical license to a graduate of a Canadian medical school who holds a license in one of the provinces of Canada. Seventeen licensing boards will, under certain specified conditions, endorse a Licentiate Medical Council of Canada certificate held by a foreign medical graduate.

In the most recent survey (June, 1979) conducted by the AMA Department of Physician Credentials and Qualification, forty-seven states have indicated they will license foreign medical graduates who hold a Fifth Pathway certificate.

Foreign educated candidates for licensure are permitted by twenty-two state boards to take the FLEX before they have had graduate training. In most cases, however, candidates are not awarded a license until they have undertaken one or two years of training in the U.S. and have met other specific requirements of the individual boards, e.g., an Educational Commission on Foreign Medical Graduates (ECFMG) certificate, personal interview, etc.

Tables 8F-1, 8F-2, and 8F-3 on the following pages summarize the licensure policies of state boards. It is strongly recommended that candidates contact the specific state board for the most current information on licensure requirements in that state. Names and addresses of the corresponding officers are listed in Exhibit 8F-1 of this appendix.

RESTRICTED LICENSES AND EDUCATIONAL PERMITS

Forty-eight boards provide for the issuance of educational permits, limited and temporary licenses, or other certificates for the restricted practice of medicine. The terms for the issuance of such certificates vary. Such certificates may be issued (1) for hospital training of those eligible for licensure, (2) for supervised employment in state or private hospitals, and (3) for fulltime practice until the next regular session of the licensing board. These permits must generally be renewed once a year with a stipulated maximum number of renewals allowed (usually five years).

VISA QUALIFYING EXAMINATION

Amendments to the Immigration and Nationality Act made through Public Law 94-484, the Health Professions Educational Assistance Act of 1976, establish new requirements for the admission of alien physicians to the United States, whether for permanent residency or for participation in graduate medical education training programs. The amendments require that alien graduates of foreign medical schools pass Parts I and II of the National Board of Medical Examiners examination, or an examination determined by the Secretary of Health, Education, and Welfare, to be the equivalent. The amendments also require that alien medical graduates demonstrate competence in oral and written English.

The Secretary of Health, Education, and Welfare has determined that the Visa Qualifying Examination (VQE), which is prepared by the National Board of Medical Examiners and administered by the Educational Commission for Foreign Medical Graduates, is the equivalent of Parts I and II of the National Board of Medical Examiners examination for purposes of the amendments to the Immigration and Nationality Act. This examination, which lasts for two days and is composed of equal proportions of clinical science and basic science questions in a multiple choice format, is given once a year at a limited number of examination centers abroad and in the United States. Applications for the examination and questions should be addressed to the Educational Commission for Foreign Medical Graduates, 3624 Market Street, Philadelphia, Pa. 19104, U.S.A.

The new amendments to the Immigration and Nationality Act are not applicable to graduates of foreign medical schools who are citizens of the United States, are already lawful permanent residents of the United States, or who seek such residence as the parents, spouses, children, brothers, or sisters of United States citizens, or as the spouses or unmarried children of lawful permanent residency aliens of the United States. Questions concerning whether an alien medical graduate is required to take the VQE should be addressed to American Embassies and Consulates General abroad.

Table 8F-1 Policies of State Boards of Medical Examiners for Initial Licensure for Graduates of U.S. Medical Schools

State	Written exam	Endorsement of national boards (NB)	Length of time NBs are endorsed	Graduate training required	No. of yrs. of graduate training required
Alabama	Yes	Yes	NL	Yes	1
Alaska	Yes	Yes	NL	Yes	1
Arizona	Yes	Yes	15 yrs. (See[3])	Yes	1
Arkansas	Yes	Yes	..	No[2]	0
California	Yes	Yes	..	Yes	1
Colorado	Yes	Yes	NL	Yes	1
Connecticut	Yes	Yes	..	Yes	2
Delaware	Yes	Yes	NL	Yes	1
District of Columbia	Yes	Yes	NL	Yes	1

Table 8F-1 continued

State	Written exam	Endorsement of national boards (NB)	Length of time NBs are endorsed	Graduate training required	No. of yrs. of graduate training required
Florida	Yes	Yes	10 yrs.	Yes	1 yr.[5]
Georgia	Yes	Yes	NL	Yes	1
Guam	No	Yes	..	Yes	0
Hawaii	Yes	Yes	NL	Yes	1
Idaho	Yes	Yes	NL	Yes	1
Illinois	Yes	Yes[4]	NL	Yes	1
Indiana	Yes	Yes	NL	No	0
Iowa	Yes	Yes	NL	Yes	1
Kansas	Yes	Yes	..	Yes	1
Kentucky	Yes	Yes	NL	Yes	1
Louisiana	Yes	No	..	No	0
Maine	Yes	Yes	NL	Yes	1
Maryland	Yes	Yes	..	No	0
Massachusetts	Yes	Yes	NL	No	0
Michigan	Yes	Yes	..	Yes	1
Minnesota	Yes	Yes	NL	Yes[2]	1
Mississippi	Yes	Yes	NL	No[4]	0
Missouri	Yes	Yes	..	No	0
Montana	Yes	Yes	..	Yes	1
Nebraska	Yes	Yes	NL	Yes[2]	1
Nevada	Yes[3]	Yes[3]	NL	Yes	1
New Hampshire	Yes	Yes	..	Yes[2 3]	2
New Jersey	Yes	Yes	NL	Yes	1
New Mexico	Yes	Yes	..	No	0
New York	Yes	Yes	NL	No	0
North Carolina	Yes	Yes	NL	Yes	1
North Dakota	Yes	Yes	NL	Yes	1
Ohio	Yes	Yes	NL	No	0
Oklahoma	Yes	Yes	(See[2])	Yes[1]	1
Oregon	Yes	Yes	NL	Yes	1
Pennsylvania	Yes	Yes	NL	Yes	1
Puerto Rico	Yes	Yes	..	Yes	0
Rhode Island	Yes	Yes	NL	Yes	1
South Carolina	Yes	Yes	NL	Yes	1
South Dakota	Yes	Yes	NL	Yes	1
Tennessee	Yes	Yes	..	No	0
Texas	Yes	No	..	No	0
Utah	Yes	Yes	NL	Yes	1
Vermont	Yes	Yes	NL	Yes	1
Virgin Islands	Yes	No	..	Yes	1
Virginia	Yes	Yes	..	Yes	1
Washington	Yes	Yes	NL	Yes	1
West Virginia	Yes	Yes	8 yrs.	Yes	1
Wisconsin	Yes	Yes	NL	Yes	1
Wyoming	Yes	Yes	NL	No	0

No—Implies no or not required.
NL—Indicates No limit.
[1] First year residency accepted except in pathology and psychiatry.
[2] At the discretion of the board.
[3] Oral examination required.
[4] Oral interview required.
[5] Or 5 years licensed practice.

Table 8F–2 Policies of State Boards of Medical Examiners for Citizens of Canada Who Are Graduates of Approved Canadian Medical Schools*

State	Certification by Medical Council of Canada approved for licensure by reciprocity or endorsement	Canadian internship accepted as equivalent to first-year graduate training served in a U.S. hospital
Alabama	Yes	Yes
Alaska	Yes	Yes[f]
Arizona	Yes	Yes
Arkansas	Yes	Yes
California	No	Yes
Colorado	No	Yes
Connecticut	Yes	Yes
Delaware	Yes	Yes
District of Columbia	No	Yes
Florida	No	Yes
Georgia	Yes	Yes
Guam	Yes	. .
Hawaii	No	Yes
Idaho	No	Yes
Illinois	Yes	Yes
Indiana	Yes	Yes
Iowa	Yes[a]	. .
Kansas	Yes	Yes
Kentucky	Yes	Yes
Louisiana	No	(See[d])
Maine	Yes	Yes
Maryland	No[c]	No[d]
Massachusetts	Yes[d]	No[d]
Michigan	No	Yes
Minnesota	Yes	Yes
Mississippi	Yes	Yes
Missouri	No	(See[d])
Montana	Yes	Yes
Nebraska	Yes	Yes
Nevada	No	Yes
New Hampshire	Yes	Yes[g]
New Jersey	No	Yes[f]
New Mexico	Yes	. .
New York	Yes[a]	Yes
North Carolina	No	Yes
North Dakota	Yes	Yes
Ohio	No	No[c]
Oklahoma	No	Yes
Oregon	Yes	Yes
Pennsylvania	No	Yes
Puerto Rico	No	. .
Rhode Island	Yes[b]	Yes[b]
South Carolina	No	Yes
South Dakota	Yes	Yes
Tennessee	Yes	(See[d])

Table 8F–2 continued

State	Certification by Medical Council of Canada approved for licensure by reciprocity or endorsement	Canadian internship accepted as equivalent to first-year graduate training served in a U.S. hospital
Texas	Yes[a]	Yes
Utah	Yes	Yes
Vermont	No	Yes
Virgin Islands	No	Yes[f]
Virginia	Yes	..
Washington	No	Yes
West Virginia	Yes	Yes
Wisconsin	Yes[h]	Yes
Wyoming	No[e]	Yes

*All State Boards of Medical Examiners consider Canadian citizens who have graduated from an approved Canadian medical school, on the same basis for licensure as graduates of approved U.S. medical schools.

[a] Must be endorsed by provincial licensing Board.

[b] By vote of Board.

[c] On an individual basis if not also American Board Certified for Maryland.

[d] Training not required.

[e] Only FLEX.

[f] If approved by Canadian Medical Association or AMA.

[g] Two years postgraduate training required.

[h] If taken after 1/1/78.

.. Did not respond.

Table 8F–3 Policies of State Boards of Medical Examiners for Physicians Trained in Foreign Countries Other Than Canada

State	Permits Partial Retake of FLEX	ECFMG Certificate	Permits Candidate to Take FLEX Without U.S. Training	U.S. Graduate Training Required to Obtain License	Examination Fees
Alabama	No	Yes	No	Yes	$150
Alaska	Yes	Yes	No	..	150
Arizona	No	Yes	No	Yes	200
Arkansas	No	Yes	Yes	Yes	125
California	Yes	No	Yes	Yes	100
Colorado	No	Yes	Yes	Yes	99
Connecticut	Yes	No	No	Yes	150
Delaware	No	Yes	No	Yes	240
District of Columbia	No	Yes	No	Yes	200

Table 8F–3 continued

State	Permits Partial Retake of FLEX	ECFMG Certificate	Permits Candidate to Take FLEX Without U.S. Training	U.S. Graduate Training Required to Obtain License	Examination Fees
Florida	No	Yes	Yes	Yes	175
Georgia	No	No	Yes	Yes	200
Guam	Yes	Yes	Yes	..	150
Hawaii	No	Yes	No	Yes	125
Idaho	No	Yes	No	Yes	200
Illinois	Yes	No	No	Yes	75
Indiana	No	No	Yes	Yes	150
Iowa	No	Yes	Yes	Yes	100
Kansas	No	Yes	No	Yes	100
Kentucky	No	Yes	Yes	Yes	150
Louisiana	No	Yes	No	Yes	150
Maine	Yes	Yes	No	Yes	175
Maryland	No	Yes	No	Yes	155
Massachusetts	No	Yes	Yes	No	125
Michigan	Yes	Yes	No	Yes	165
Minnesota	Yes	Yes	Yes	..	125
Mississippi	No	Yes	No	Yes	175
Missouri	No	Yes	No	Yes	50
Montana	No	Yes	Yes	Yes	100
Nebraska	No	Yes	No	Yes	150
Nevada	No	No	No	Yes	200
New Hampshire	Yes	Yes	No	Yes	150
New Jersey	Yes	No	No	Yes	150
New Mexico	No	Yes	Yes	No	100
New York	Yes	Yes	No	Yes	100
North Carolina	No	Yes	Yes	Yes	150
North Dakota	Yes	Yes	Yes	Yes	150
Ohio	No	Yes	No	Yes	125
Oklahoma	Yes	Yes	Yes	Yes	200
Oregon	Yes	Yes	Yes	Yes	150[1]
Pennsylvania	No	Yes	No	Yes	150
Puerto Rico	Yes	No	Yes	..	30
Rhode Island	No	Yes	No	Yes	150
South Carolina	Yes	Yes	No	Yes	175
South Dakota	Yes	Yes	No	Yes	150
Tennessee	No	Yes	No	Yes	150
Texas	Yes	Yes	Yes	No	150
Utah	No	Yes	No	Yes	100
Vermont	No	Yes	Yes	Yes	200
Virgin Islands	No	Yes	No	Yes	100
Virginia	Yes	Yes	No	Yes	175
Washington	No	Yes	No	No	100
West Virginia	No	Yes	Yes	Yes	150
Wisconsin	No	Yes	No	Yes	50
Wyoming	Yes	Yes	Yes		150

Yes—Implies yes.
No—Implies no or not required.
[1] Plus the cost of FLEX.

Exhibit 8F-1 Corresponding Officers of Boards of Medical Examiners in the United States and Possessions

---

Alabama: Executive Secretary, Alabama State Board of Medical Examiners, P.O. Box 946, Montgomery 36102.

Alaska: Licensing Examiner, Department of Commerce & Economic Development, Division of Occupational Licensing, State Medical Board, Pouch D, Juneau 99811.

Arizona: Executive Director, Arizona Board of Medical Examiners, 5060 N. 19th Avenue, Suite 300, Phoenix 85013.

Arkansas: Secretary, Arkansas State Medical Board, P.O. Box 102, Harrisburg 72432.

California: Executive Secretary. California Board of Medical Quality Assurance, 1430 Howe Ave., Sacramento 95825.

Colorado: Secretary to the Board, Board of Medical Examiners, 1525 Sherman Street, Room 132, Denver 80202.

Connecticut: Executive Director, Board of Medical Examiners, 79 Elm St., Hartford 06115.

Delaware: Board of Medical Practice of Delaware, Board of Medical Examiners, Margaret O'Neill Bldg., Box 1401, Dover 19901.

District of Columbia: Commission on Licensure, 614 H St., NW, Washington, D.C. 20001.

Florida: Executive Director, Board of Medical Examiners, 130 N. Monroe Street, Tallahassee 32301.

Georgia: Executive Director, Composite State Board of Medical Examiners, 166 Pryor Street, S.W., Room 300, Atlanta 30303.

Guam: Commission on Licensure to Practice the Healing Art, Guam Memorial Hospital, P.O. Box AX, Marianas Islands, Agana 96910.

Hawaii: Board of Medical Examiners, P.O. Box 541, Honolulu 96809.

Idaho: Executive Secretary, State Board of Medicine, P.O. Box 6817, Boise 83707.

Illinois: Director, Department of Registration and Education, 320 W. Washington, Springfield 62786.

Indiana: Medical Licensing Board of Indiana, 700 N. High School Road, Suite 201, Indianapolis 46224.

Iowa: Executive Director, Board of Medical Examiners, State Capitol Complex, Executive Hills West, Des Moines 50319.

Kansas: Executive Secretary, Board of Medical Examiners, 503 Kansas Avenue, Suite 500, Topeka 66603.

Kentucky: Ass't. Secretary, State Board of Medical Licensure, 3532 Ephraim McDowell Drive, Louisville 40205.

Louisiana: Secretary-Treasurer, Louisiana State Board of Medical Examiners. 830 Union Street, Suite 100, New Orleans 70112

Maine: Executive Secretary, Board of Medical Examiners, 100 College Avenue, Waterville 04901.

Maryland: Board of Medical Examiners, 201 W. Preston Street, 5th Floor, Baltimore 21201.

Massachusetts: Secretary, Massachusetts Board of Registration & Discipline in Medicine, 100 Cambridge St., Room 1511, Boston 02202.

Michigan: Execuitve Director, Michigan Board of Medicine, 905 Southland, P.O. Box 30018, Lansing 48909

Minnesota: Executive Secretary, Board of Medical Examiners, 717 Delaware St., S.E., Room 352, Minneapolis 55414.

Exhibit 8F-1 continued

Mississippi: Asst. State Hlth. Officer for Licensure, State Board of Health, P.O. Box 1700, Jackson 39205.

Missouri: Executive Secretary, Board of Registration for the Healing Arts, P.O. Box 4, Jefferson City 65102.

Montana: Secretary, Board of Medical Examiners, LaLonde Bldg., Helena 59601.

Nebraska: Exec. Secretary, State Board of Examiners in Medicine, 301 Centennial Mall South, P.O. Box 95007, Lincoln 68509.

Nevada: Board of Medical Examiners, P.O. Box 7238, Reno 89510.

New Hampshire: Executive Secretary, Board of Registration Medicine, Health & Welfare Building, Hazen Drive, Concord 03301.

New Jersey: Executive Secretary, Board of Medical Examiners, 28 W. State, Trenton 08608.

New Mexico: Executive Secretary, Board of Medical Examiners, 227 E. Palace Ave., Santa Fe 87501.

New York: Executive Secretary, New York Board of Medical Examiners, State Education Department, Empire State Plaza, Cultural Education Center, Albany, 12230.

North Carolina: Executive Secretary, North Carolina Board of Medical Examiners, Suite 214, 222 N. Person St., Raleigh 27601.

North Dakota: Executive Secretary, 418 E. Rosser, Bismarck 58501.

Ohio: Administrator, Board of Medical Examiners, 65 Front St., Suite 510, Columbus 43215.

Oklahoma: Executive Secretary, Board of Medical Examiners, P.O. Box 18256, Suite C, Oklahoma City 73154.

Oregon: Executive Secretary, Board of Medical Examiners, 1002 Loyalty Bldg., 317 S. W. Alder St., Portland 97204.

Pennsylvania: Secretary, Board of Medical Education and Licensure, Box 2649, 279 Boas St., Harrisburg 17120.

Puerto Rico: Secretary, Board of Medical Examiners, Box 3271, San Juan 00907.

Rhode Island: Administrator, 104 Cannon Building, 75 Davis Street, Providence 02908.

South Carolina: Executive Director, Board of Medical Examiners, 1315 Blanding St., Columbia 29201.

South Dakota: Executive Secretary, Board of Medical and Osteopathic Examiners, 608 West Ave., North Sioux Falls 57104.

Tennessee: Secretary, Tennessee Board of Medical Examiners, R.S. Gass S.O.B., Ben Allen Road, Nashville 37216.

Texas: Secretary, Board of Medical Examiners, 211 East 7, Suite 900, Austin 78701.

Utah: Director, Department of Registration, 330 E. 4th South, Salt Lake City 84111.

Vermont: Secretary, Board of Medical Practice, 13 Baldwin St., Montpelier 06502.

Virgin Islands: Office of the Commissioner of Health, St. Thomas 00801.

Virginia: Executive Secretary, State Board of Medicine, 3600 W. Broad St., Suite 453, Richmond 23220.

Washington: Professional Licensing Division, Box 9649, Olympia 98504.

West Virginia: Secretary, Medical Licensing Board, 1800 Washington St., Charleston 25305.

Wisconsin: Board of Medical Examiners, 1400 E. Washington Ave., Madison 53702.

Wyoming: Board of Medical Examiners, Hathaway Bldg., 4th Floor, Cheyenne 82002.

Chapter 9

Location Preferences

After the recruitment committee has reviewed all the possible sources for physicians, it can initiate the screening of individuals for site visits and interviews.

What are the chances that a physician will select one community over another to visit? What motivational factors will influence a physician's decision to relocate to a specific area? Interest in the factors that influence these location decisions has increased due to the overall maldistribution of physicians in the country. As the recruitment process continues, it becomes critically important to understand the variables that govern the selection of a physician practice location.

KEY FACTORS

The literature on physician location is both voluminous and difficult to synthesize. Many different studies show a wide range of factors that influence a physician's selection of a practice location. However, a consensus of research indicates that there are five major categories of influence on the selection of physician location. Rather than select one key factor, we should be aware that all five of the following factors contribute to a physician's choice:

1. *prior exposure*—those events in the life of the physician that have allowed him to have contact with a community
2. *environmental factors*—those attributes that contribute to the quality of life in a community: cultural and social opportunities, the educational system, the quality of the community
3. *medical environment*—those practice-related aspects contributing to a satisfying professional life: hospitals, medical schools, patient referral patterns, and office space

4. *economic factors*—those factors influencing practice net income directly: financial arrangements, gross income, costs, excess demands
5. *demand determinants*—those demographic and economic attributes of
   an area that affect the demand for health services (i.e., population size,
   sex, race, income, educational attainment)[1]

Prior Exposure

A study in 1966 indicated that physicians located their first practice in
areas where significant events in their lives had occurred. Places of birth and
where the physician attended medical school, internship, and residency were
reported to play a significant role in the practice determination.[2] A major
drawback of this study was that there was little if any information on motivational factors. Also overlooked were those physicians who located in areas
with which they had no previous contact.

More recent research has indicated that early socialization in an environment is a stronger determinant of practice location than more recent professional socialization. This held true specifically for primary care physicians; it
was not true of specialists. In the vital training years, physicians tend to be
taken away from rural settings and inducted into more specialized medicine.
For the most part, these experiences diminish incentives to return to a rural
practice. If such training produces a specialist, the option of a rural practice
is in fact largely ignored.[3]

Lack of knowledge about a geographical area may also cause a physician
to exclude an area as a practice location. Indeed, the geographic distribution
of physicians reflects the availability, reliability, and nature of the information regarding the selection of a practice location.[4]

It is important to provide the physician with positive exposure and information regarding the community. By educating the physician about a community in the preinterview and interview process, the possibility of a
relocation is maximized.

Environmental Factors

Since the majority of people are concerned with the quality of life in a
community, it is important to highlight those aspects that make a community special. A recent study has demonstrated that a community's schools and
its cultural and recreational opportunities are the biggest factors in a physician's location decision. These were more important than financial considerations, family ties, climate, or a community's need for physicians.[5] Though
this contradicts previous research, it is possible that physicians base their
decisions on opportunities for a good family environment and a high quality

of life. Rural communities can utilize this factor to its advantage by high-lighting the positive aspects of a small rural town, emphasizing lower crime rates, less congestion, and a rewarding community life. In short, a presentation of the positive attributes of the community environment can greatly affect a physician's decision to locate in the community.

Medical Environment

A physician looking for a practice location will be strongly influenced by the medical environment. Of primary concern will be what type of hospital the physician will be affiliated with and if the facilities and equipment are sophisticated. Who are the other physicians in the area, and what will the referral patterns be like? Is office space available? Answers to these questions can have a dramatic effect on the decision of a physician in choosing a practice location.

Research has indicated that specialist physicians in particular place an emphasis on the quality of the medical environment, relative to other considerations. Specialists are attracted by the availability of hospitals, access to sophisticated equipment, and the presence of medical schools and teaching hospitals.[6] The recruitment committee should be prepared to present this type of information on the medical community to the visiting physician.

Economic Factors

Economic factors will have a strong impact on a physician's choice of location. Research has indicated that the general economic condition of an area is the number one factor in the location decision of physicians.[7]

Another significant economic factor is the type of financial arrangement the hospital offers the physician. When a physician completes his training, it is possible that he will have incurred debts for his medical education. This financial need will definitely impact on which practice opportunity the physician will choose. Thus, as the practice opportunity is presented, the financial arrangements and potential income that the situation has to offer should be highlighted.

Demand Determinants

A physician who is looking for a practice location will be strongly influenced by the demand for his services. A primary concern will be whether the demographics of the area can support the incoming physician's medical practice. For example, one study has indicated that the most important single factor affecting the geographic distribution of physicians is population.[8]

Table 9–1 Factors Influencing the Location Decisions of Established Practitioners and Students

Factor	Students Final Rank[a]	Students Mean Rank[b]	Current Practitioners Final Rank[a]	Current Practitioners Mean Rank[b]
Preference for small community and culture	1	4.0	7	9.0
Rural preceptorship for students with rural background (this was judged to be of no value for students from urban areas)	2	4.6	—	—
Potential for rapid practice growth	3	5.3	4	5.2
Availability of group practice	4	5.8	8	9.7
Spouse's attitude	5	7.7	1	3.7
Community orientation of practice	6	8.2	5	6.8
Assistance in cost of capital investment of practice establishment	7	8.4	10	10.3
Activities for spouse	8	9.6	6	7.4
Location of residency	9	10.2	12	12.1
Close (one hour) proximity to a major cultural and shopping center	10	11.2	9	10.1
Availability of peer professional manpower	11	11.2	3	4.6
Available facilities	12	11.6	2	3.9
Availability of cultural activities	13	11.7	18	15.3
Orientation of professional education to problem	14	12.3	—	—
Location of internship	15	13.3	16	13.5
Recreational activities	16	13.6	11	11.6
Positive financial incentives to locate in underserved areas	17	14.8	—	—
Professional school curriculum that relates to primary care and underserved area problems	18	15.0	—	—
Family attitude	19	15.6	17	15.0
Availability of specialist manpower	20	17.3	15	13.5
Per capita income	—	—	13	12.2
Rural location of primary and high school education	—	—	14	12.7
Advice, location of friends	—	—	19	15.8
Community prestige and opportunities for community leadership	—	—	20	17.0

[a] Indicates how the experts ranked a factor as an influence on the practice location decision for students or current practitioners.
[b] Average rank assigned by the group of experts participating in the study.

Source: " 'Expert' Opinion of the Most Important Factors Influencing the Location Decisions of Established Practitioners and Students," *Journal of Medical Education* 52 (© September 1977): 772. Used by permission.

Table 9-2 Factors Influencing the Location Decision of Primary Care Physicians

Factor	Number	Percent
Opportunity to join a desirable partnership or group practice	499	43.0
Climate or geographic features of area	402	34.6
Availability of clinical support facilities and personnel	251	21.6
Preference for urban or rural living	250	21.5
Income potential	192	16.5
Opportunity for regular contact with a medical school or medical center	184	15.9
Influence of wife or husband (her/his desires, career, etc.)	181	15.6
Having been brought up in such a community	163	14.0
Having gone through medical school, internship, residency, or military service near area	143	12.3
Recreational and sports facilities	139	12.0
High medical need in area	136	11.7
Quality of educational system for children	119	10.3
Opportunity of regular contact with other physicians	113	9.7
Influence of family or friends	107	9.2
Access to continuing education	103	8.9
Cultural advantages	91	7.8
Opportunity to work with specific institution	68	5.9
Opportunities for social life	40	3.5
Prosperity of community	30	2.6
Organized efforts of community to recruit physicians	22	1.9
Advice of older physician	21	1.8
Prospect of being more influential in community affairs	20	1.7
Influence of preceptorship program	12	1.0
Payment of forgiveness loan	11	1.0
Availability of good social service, welfare, or home care services	11	1.0
Availability of loans for beginning practice	9	0.8

Note: N=161

Source: J.K. Cooper, K. Heald, M. Samuels, and S. Coleman, "Rural or Urban Practice: Factors Influencing the Location Decision of Primary Care Physicians," Table 3. Reprinted with permission of The Blue Cross Association, from *Inquiry*, vol. XII, no. 1 (March 1975), p. 20. © 1975 by The Blue Cross Association. All rights reserved.

In choosing a location, physicians have tended to follow population movements. Not surprisingly, there appears to be a threshold population that is necessary to support a physician. This may explain the lack of active primary care physicians in many sparsely populated areas in the United States.

The market analysis performed in the planning stages of the physician recruitment program will provide the necessary population information to present to a physician who is interested in a community.

SUMMARY

It is important to realize that there are many potential influences that bear upon the selection of a physician location. The studies we have cited emphasize different primary reasons why a physician would prefer a given community. Table 9-1 shows the relative importance of the different factors in influencing the location decisions of established practitioners and students, based on a 1977 study. Table 9-2 shows the frequency of location factors ranked by primary care physicians, as reported in a 1975 study. Together, these two tables show the relative importance of the many factors that influence physician location. The most significant positive factors of the community, hospital, and practice opportunity should be incorporated into the initial contact stage of the preinterview with the physician candidate.

NOTES

1. John McFarland, "The Physician's Location Decision," in *Profile of Medical Practice, 1973,* ed. Steve G. Vahovich (Chicago: American Medical Association, 1973), pp. 89–96.

2. Ibid., p. 90.

3. Donald L. Madison, "Managing a Chronic Problem: The Rural Physician Shortage," *Annals of Internal Medicine,* June 1980, pp. 852–854.

4. McFarland, "Physician's Location Decision," p. 93.

5. Susan LaVoilette, "Physicians Locate Where Benefits Best," *Modern Health Care,* March 1979, p. 34.

6. McFarland, "Physician's Location Decision," p. 93.

7. Ibid., p. 91.

8. James R. Cantwell, "Economic Factors Affecting Physician Location," in *Socioeconomic Issues of Health, 1975–1976,* ed. Henry R. Mason (Chicago: American Medical Association, 1976), p. 26.

Chapter 10

The Preinterview Process

BASIC STEPS

The head of the recruitment committee will decide which committee members will be active in the preinterview process. Regardless of who has the responsibility, however, the steps will be the same: initial contact, telephone call, prescreening, and follow-up.

Initial Contacts

The practice opportunity should be advertised in several journals and newspapers. The physicians who respond to the advertisements will contact the recruitment committee. The committee should also contact physicians whose names are listed in the placement bulletins of local medical associations and journals. Finally, the committee should contact any physician who is referred by local physicians or located through a residency or fellowship program.

Telephone Calls

In contacting the physician candidate, the committee should determine if he is committed to a position, is considering several different opportunities or is not presently considering other alternatives. If the physician indicates that he is committed to another situation, the committee should continue to discuss the situation with him, presenting the opportunity in a strong, positive manner. In response, the physician might either indicate interest in the opportunity himself or recommend a colleague for the position.

Many administrators make the mistake of ascertaining interest but then not pursuing the interest adequately. A physician is in a very vulnerable spot in making a location decision, especially if he is just completing residency. Although he may have made a choice earlier in his career, he may now have some uncertainties and will need more information on additional alternatives. Thus, the committee should be persistent and not allow an initial negative answer to terminate a telephone call.

Once a level of interest has been established, the contact should begin with an indepth discussion of the practice situation. There are many different views about this step in the preinterviewing process. Many professional recruiters feel that a minimum of information should be presented at this point and that the physician should be encouraged to do most of the talking. We have found, however, that successful physician recruitment usually depends on an equal exchange of information. The initial telephone call is the perfect opportunity to explain in great detail the practice opportunity.

The market analysis will have generated information that is relevant to the physician. This information can be utilized to sway a physician into considering one community instead of another. In this context, the physician should be encouraged to ask questions regarding the practice, hospital, and community. These questions will help to establish a profile of the physician. If the first questions raised relate to the financial commitment and arrangements that a community is willing to provide, perhaps the physician is too eager to take the position for the wrong reasons. If, instead, the physician asks questions about the medical environment and how it relates to the community, he may be demonstrating a genuine interest in the community. The key is to try to interpret the intent of his questions. In this way, the candidate can be evaluated and it can be determined whether or not an area visit is warranted. Also, during this exchange of information, the interest of the physician's spouse can be determined.

It is important to ask why the physician is relocating. If the physician is finishing a residency program, the reason is obvious. Unless he chooses to stay at that institution to pursue a fellowship or become involved in research, he will have to start a practice. This question is particularly critical if the physician is presently in practice and has decided to move. The reason for the intended move must be determined early in the conversation so that the committee member can be aware of it as the preinterviewing process continues. In this way, if any inconsistencies develop during the conversation, the interviewer will be able to address the issue. This, however, should be done in a tactful manner; the physician might be medically well qualified but be embarrassed by the reason for his move.

Up to this point, the discussion has been about the available situation. The interviewer can now gain insight into a physician's needs by asking him to describe his ideal practice situation. In this way, the interviewer can determine if the physician is compatible with the practice opportunity.

Exhibit 10-1 presents a list of questions by category that can be used to elicit information about a physician candidate in the initial telephone call. A supplemental questionnaire is provided in Exhibit 10-2. These questions will solicit much of the information that is necessary to determine whether or not an area visit is appropriate. Because it is easy to forget salient points when presenting the practice opportunity, these questions should be kept available for reference throughout the telephone conversation.

Prescreening

An indepth prescreening process, which many times can be conducted during the initial telephone call, can ensure that the physician who visits the community is qualified and compatible with the community's needs. Because the physicians who are brought to the community will be carefully selected and represent the highest calibre of applicants, the indepth screening will also promote enthusiasm among those involved in the recruitment process. If there is no prescreening, there will necessarily be a need for more physician area visits. However, many of these visiting physician candidates will not have the qualifications or interest level that the community desires. In this case, the most active recruitment supporters may begin to lose interest in volunteering their time because they will feel their efforts are being wasted.

It should be determined whether the physician's qualifications and personal and medical profile are compatible with the practice opportunity. In this regard, if a thorough prescreening is performed during the initial telephone call, a great deal of time and embarrassment can be saved. There is nothing more disappointing than to talk with a physician for a period of time, to invite him out to the community, and to spend valuable time with him and his wife only to find that obvious considerations prevent him from relocating to the community.

The candidate's curriculum vitae should be requested so that preliminary credential checks can be conducted. The medical school, residency, and other credentials should be verified prior to an area visit. Guidelines for credential checking are presented in Appendix 10-A.

The last step in the prescreening process is to obtain a commitment of interest. After the recruitment committee member has summarized the situation with the physician, discussing the good points of the community and practice, it is important to determine the physician's level of interest. A quality interaction concludes with a summary of the discussion, so that the interviewer and the physician are certain of the next step. If the physician has responded in a positive manner, the succeeding steps should be expedited. If the physician appears to be a qualified candidate, an area visit should be scheduled as soon as possible. The area visit should be arranged so that

Exhibit 10-1 Candidate Information Sheet

General Information about the Candidate
1. Name
2. Address
3. Phone
4. Medical school
5. Residency
6. References
7. Associations
8. Licenses

Candidate's Environmental Needs
1. Size of community
2. Climate
3. Recreation orientation
4. Schools for children
5. Schools for spouse
6. Friends—where located

Candidate's Financial Concerns
1. Needs assistance
2. Income guarantee
3. Expectations

Candidate's Medical Interests
1. Other physicians with whom the candidate wishes to practice
2. Type of practice (solo, group, partnership)

the committee will have sufficient time to prepare for the visit. Information should be forwarded to the physician regarding the practice, hospital, and community so that he can review the material prior to the area visit. The physician should be contacted one week after the initial contact to confirm the area visit and to discuss the proposed itinerary.

If the physician is not interested, he should be asked what it is about the situation that is not appealing. The physician might be misinformed about certain aspects of the practice, for example, the coverage available, referral patterns, or continuing education opportunities. The interviewer should try to respond on these points in a positive manner, offering to send the physician information for review and establishing a time for a follow-up telephone

Exhibit 10-2 Physician Application Questionnaire

Eligible for state license: ☐ Yes ☐ No
Preferred distance to metropolitan area:
  ☐ 0–25 miles   ☐ 50–100 miles
  ☐ 25–50 miles   ☐ Over 100 miles

Orientation firmness:
A) Specialty   ☐ Yes   ☐ No   (Options _____)
B) Position orientation
               ☐ Yes   ☐ No   (Options _____)

Importance of schools:
A) Children   ☐ Yes   ☐ No
B) Wife   ☐ Yes   ☐ No   Type: _____

Financial:
A) Need assistance to begin practice   ☐ Yes   ☐ No
B) Income important   ☐ Yes   ☐ No
    Income guarantee $ _____
Has friends in state or area: ☐ Yes   ☐ No   (Where _____)

Other physicians with whom the physician wishes to practice:

Name: _____
Address: _____
Phone: _____
Specialty: _____
Date available: _____

Climate desired:
1) Coast   4) Mountains
2) Desert   5) Other (Specify needs) _____
3) Farmland   _____

Recreational orientation (Rank importance):
_____ Boating   _____ Fishing   _____ Golf   _____ Music
_____ Hiking   _____ Beaches   _____ Skiing   _____ Restaurants
_____ Camping   _____ Flying   _____ Theater   _____ Museums
_____ Hunting
Other comments:
Evaluation (circle appropriate number):

Interested in available practice	Some interest, relocation possible	No interest. Do not follow up
7 6 5	4 3	2 1

conversation. Circumstances have a way of changing, and persistence in pursuing the physician may yet result in a successful recruitment. Though the initial presentation of a practice opportunity may not spark the physician's interest, an informative brochure on the community and the hospital might convince him that an area visit would be worthwhile. Surprisingly many area visits have occurred following an initial negative response from a physician. The main idea is to continue a dialogue as long as possible.

A possible reaction of a physician may be to express interest but to indicate no desire actively to pursue the situation at this time. Again, the response should be to stress how the recruitment committee is actively recruiting for a physician because the need is so great. It should be explained that material will be forwarded for his review. Following his receipt of the materials, the interviewer should call to answer any additional questions he may have. This call should be made within a week of the initial contact. If the materials are sent to the physician immediately, he should have received the packet in two to three days. The follow–up within the week is especially important when working with an ambivalent physician.

The follow–up promotional information should be developed by the recruitment committee. It should positively explain the practice opportunity and be colorful and interesting. This information will hopefully interest the physician sufficiently so that he will plan an area visit to the community.

SUMMARY

The purpose of the preinterviewing process is to identify an interested physician candidate and to arrange for an area visit. Physician relocation from outside an existing area will not occur without a site visit. Utilizing basic preinterviewing skills, the hospital should be able to generate area visits that will be productive and result in physician relocation.

Appendix 10–A

Guidelines for Reference and Credentials Checks on Physicians

A. General Rules

1. Check verbally by phone all reference information that is obtained in writing. Very few people are comfortable making negative statements in writing.
2. Never limit reference checks to those given by the physician candidate.
3. If you receive information that is negative but is explained away by the person giving the information, take it as a symptom of a problem and follow through until you are satisfied that you understand the situation.
4. Do not accept references that consist of statements irrelevant to questions of professional competence and behavior. It is nice to know someone is a good boy scout leader, but that will not tell you if the person is a good doctor.
5. If possible, have a member of the medical staff make telephone calls to other physicians for reference checks, but provide a list of questions to be asked.
6. Ask for references from the administrator of the hospital where the candidate practices.
7. Never tell a candidate you are rejecting him because of references.

B. Who to Contact

1. *For physician candidates now in practice:*
   a. Start with the names given you by the candidate.
   b. Call the chiefs of staff of the hospitals where the candidate has had staff privileges.

Source: Adapted from a paper by Diane Moeller, vice president of professional services, Intermountain Health Care, Inc., Salt Lake City, Utah, at a meeting of the American Hospital Association in Miami, 1981. Used by permission.

    c. If appropriate, call the chief of the department of the hospital where the candidate presently practices.

    d. Call the president of the county medical society if the physician is a member of a medical staff with less than five members. Ask the president for another reference.

    e. If the above information is not satisfactory, for candidates in practice less than five years, contact the director of the candidate's residency program.

    f. Call the hospital administrators of the hospitals where the physician has had privileges.

    g. If you suspect problems regarding the physician's relationship with other professionals, contact the director of nursing of the hospital where the physician currently practices or a nursing supervisor of the unit the physician uses most frequently.

2. *For physician candidates completing residency programs:*

    a. Use the references given to you by the candidate.

    b. Always call the director of the residency program.

    c. As additional references, ask the director for the names of one faculty person and one attending physician who have not been submitted by the applicant.

C. Specific Questions

The following questions are meant to serve only as guidelines for a telephone conversation. The answers to these questions should, in each situation, lead to extemporaneous questions on your part. The interviewer should never give the impression of reading from a questionnaire.

1. *Questions to physicians:*

    a. Did you work with the physician as a member of the same medical staff?

        Yes _____ No _____

        If yes, continue. If no, go to questions c, g, i, j, and k.

    b. Did you personally ever have reason to question the physician's medical/surgical competence?

        Yes _____ No _____

        If yes, ask for an explanation.

    c. Are you aware of committees of the medical staff ever having considered or having actually taken action against the physician for poor medical practice?

        Yes _____ No _____

    d. Have you heard of concerns expressed by the medical staff over the quality of the physician's practice?

        Yes _____ No _____

If yes, ask for an explanation.

e. Does the physician work well with other members of the medical staff?

Yes _____ No _____

If no, ask for an explanation.

f. Does the physician participate actively in medical staff affairs?

Yes _____ No _____

If no, ask for an explanation.

g. Has the physician been an officer of the medical staff or accepted chairmanship of any committees?

Yes _____ No _____

If no, ask for an explanation.

h. Do you and/or other members of the medical community consider the physician a medical staff leader?

Yes _____ No _____

If no, ask for an explanation.

i. Does the physician relate well and in a professional manner with members of the hospital employee staff?

Yes _____ No _____

If no, ask for an explanation.

j. Does the physician have a physical or mental illness that might interfere with his professional performance?

Yes _____ No _____

If yes, ask for an explanation.

k. Does the physician have, or has he had in the past, any personal problems, e.g., alcoholism or drug abuse, that might interfere with his professional practice?

Yes _____ No _____

If yes, ask for an explanation.

l. Does the physician have a large medical practice?

Yes _____ No _____

m. Has the physician ever lost admitting privileges because of incomplete records?

Yes _____ No _____

If yes, ask for an explanation.

2. *Questions to hospital administrators and other hospital personnel:*

a. Have you ever received reports of poor medical practice by the physician or have you discussed with medical staff officers any concerns you had about the quality of his practice?

Yes _____ No _____

If yes, ask for an explanation.

b. Have you received reports of poor relationships between the physician and other members of the hospital staff?
   Yes _____ No _____
   If yes, ask for an explanation.

c. Does the physician accept medical staff policy and function willingly according to this policy?
   Yes _____ No _____
   If no, ask for an explanation.

d. Does the physician complete his medical records in a timely manner and in such a way as to protect the hospital legally?
   Yes _____ No _____
   If no, ask for an explanation.

e. Does the physician have any medical or physical problems that might interfere with his practice in the hospital?
   Yes _____ No _____
   If yes, ask for an explanation.

f. Does the physician have any personal habits that might interfere with his practice in the hospital, e.g., drug abuse, alcoholism, etc.
   Yes _____ No _____
   If yes, ask for an explanation.

g. About what percentage of admissions to your hospital do you attribute to the physician? _____

h. Are you sorry to see the physician leave your community?
   Yes _____ No _____
   If no, ask for an explanation.

Chapter 11

The Interview Process

BASIC ELEMENTS

After the prescreening process has been completed, the site visit and the interview process can proceed. There are eight basic elements in a successful interview with a physician candidate:

1. development of an itinerary
2. initial meeting
3. community tour
4. interview with the administrator
5. interview with medical staff
6. hospital tour
7. social activities
8. commitment to the candidate

The head of the recruitment committee should determine which individual will be responsible for each of the above elements. It should be remembered that each community and situation is unique, and the committee should modify and augment each element as necessary.

Development of an Itinerary

A complete and well-constructed itinerary can be the difference between an excellent and a mediocre physician area visit. Since a large percentage of the physicians interviewed will be married, much of the itinerary will involve concerns and activities specifically related to the physician's spouse.

After the physician agrees to a visit, the amount of time that the physician can spend in the community should be determined. It is best to have the candidate arrive on a Friday so that a full weekend is available for the visit. The Friday evening can be social, leaving Saturday for business meetings.

The Saturday evening can be devoted to a social event, and Sunday the physician can spend touring the area.

If the physician is flying or driving in from another area, the appropriate reservations and hotel accommodations must be secured well in advance. Arrangements should be made for the physician to stay at a better hotel in town and for a car to be available. If the physician chooses to make his own flight reservations, the meeting with his escort should be coordinated with the exact time of arrival. If the committee is responsible for the flight, the flight arrangements should be made as soon as possible so that the physician will have the tickets far in advance of the visit.

The area visit should be verified two days prior to the visit to confirm the physician's interest level and the fact that he is indeed planning to visit. Nothing can be more disappointing than to arrange an entire recruiting weekend only to find out at the last moment that the physician has cancelled the visit.

All the individuals involved in the interviewing process should be notified in advance of the area visit, given details of the itinerary, and reminded of their individual responsibilities. To facilitate a smooth area visit, the key people should be double-checked to be sure they are aware of their tasks. Hotel and car reservations should be checked, and arrangements should be made for a bottle of wine or flowers to be in the physician's room upon his arrival.

Initial Meeting

On the visit day, the administrator should meet the physician and his family at the airport and escort them to their accommodations by the most scenic route. This is not for the purpose of concealing the community's negative points; it is meant rather to provide the physician and his spouse with a positive first impression. It is important to remember that this first impression can have a definite impact on the remainder of the visit.

The administrator should present a fully coordinated itinerary for the physician and family to follow during the visit. In this connection, it is important to arrange for someone to drive the candidate and his wife to the various meetings and events. This will help guarantee an effortless trip for the physician and allow for the best exposure to the community. During the free time available, the physician may wish to have a car at his disposal to attend to matters of special interest.

Community Tour

Though the physician has decided to visit the area because there is a practice opportunity that is of interest to him, having him *visit* the community and having him *stay* in the community are entirely different things. A physician interested in relocating is looking for a place that provides him with a good environment, social activities, and a high quality of life for himself and his family. In this regard, the recruitment committee is the key to demonstrating that the community has much to offer. Committee members should show the physician around the community, accenting those factors that influenced others to move to the area. These will probably parallel the qualities he is looking for in a community. A broad spectrum of areas—including places to live, schools, business districts, cultural spots, shopping areas, and recreational areas—should be presented. The points that make the town different from any other city should be emphasized. Careful attention to this tour will enable the physician to obtain the best view of the community and, more importantly, will enable the committee to "recruit" the spouse. If the spouse is not satisfied with the community, the chances of attracting the physician are greatly reduced.

Interview with the Administrator

During the interview with the administrator, the spouse may or may not choose to be present. The spouse's interest should be ascertained as soon as possible so that alternate plans can be made to accommodate the spouse's wishes.

The administrator is usually the key individual involved in the interview and negotiations with the physician. In the physician's interview with the administrator, the business aspects of the practice opportunity should be discussed. The two main areas that should be covered during the administrator's meetings with the physician are the specific practice opportunity and the financial considerations.

The Practice Opportunity

First, the medical community should be described in detail, utilizing the information gathered during the determining-need phase. The potential for growth and why the physician's specialty is needed in the area should be explained.

The practice specifications should be covered in detail. Is it a solo or partnership arrangement? Are there physicians currently practicing in the same specialty? Are there any problems anticipated with the physicians in the area? Possible problems should be discussed in a candid manner; covering up a tense situation can only lead to a dissatisfied and disenchanted recruited physician.

Referral patterns are extremely important to the incoming physician. The physicians who will refer to the new physician and to whom the recruited physician may wish to refer his specialty cases should be identified.

Another question is where the physician's patients will come from. Will most of them come from referring physicians, or will they come from a market that is presently going out of the community for health care? It is necessary to identify and explain the patient trend to the physician. This might be done most impressively on a graph or chart. A chart should be made for each specialty that is being recruited, showing the number of physicians presently in the community, the number of referring physicians, the number of patients in the community, and the number of those who are being lost or going elsewhere. In this way, the physician can visually see his patient base, which ultimately represents the medical practice he hopes to build in the community.

A related question, very important to the candidate, is, "Why will people in the area go to this particular physician?" The administrator must be able to answer this question in a positive manner, demonstrating the potential for the physician. If the main reason people will go to the physician is that they are currently being forced to leave the community for their health care, it should be relatively simple to convince the physician on this point. If there are other circumstances that affect the particular medical situation, it will be necessary to address these circumstances candidly and persuasively so that the physician will feel there is indeed a place for him in the community.

Another concern of the physician is the medical office space available to him. This important issue must be addressed prior to initiating the physician recruitment program. Many hospitals plan for expansion and build medical buildings on their hospital grounds. Other hospitals are not involved in the development of medical buildings and leave such projects to business concerns or physician partnerships to develop.

In either case, it will be necessary to make space available to the relocating physician. This space should be near the hospital and provide for anticipated growth. When the physician visits the community, no matter how impressive the hospital may be, he will be very concerned about the space in which he will be seeing patients on a daily basis. Many hospitals ignore this issue, or they hope that newly recruited physicians will themselves provide a financial base for a new medical building. For any of these options, it is necessary to plan ahead so that the option can be discussed when the physician is being interviewed.

The opening of an office can be a traumatic assumption of responsibility for a physician who has never been in practice before. The office equipment and furnishings, the personnel, business forms and licenses, billing procedures, and charges can all present difficult problems for the new physician. The physician should be offered expertise and assistance in dealing with these problems. The feeling by the physician that there will be individuals to guide him in these matters will serve as a strong inducement to select this particular opportunity over other similar ones.

The interview should be tailored to the physician's medical background. If the physician is a specialist, the discussion should cover plans for new sophisticated equipment or the purchase of specific equipment needed by the physician. The ancillary and support services in the hospital should also be described in detail, including how the hospital and governing board operate and the outstanding supportive characteristics of the practice opportunity.

Financial Considerations

In discussing the financial commitment of the hospital and community to the new physician, the physician should be asked what his financial situation is and what he expects from the community. The hospital's response should be tailored to the physician's needs. Even though the hospital has not officially committed itself to the physician at this point, it is important to explore these financial details. Will an office be provided rent free for six months? Will there be a six-month salary guarantee, with the physician responsible for gradual repayment of the loan? Are moving expenses to be included? The basis for answering such questions should have been established during the earlier planning committee phase, enabling the administrator at this point to address the physician's needs honestly and directly and to present the financial package in the most positive light. (For a detailed examination of the hospital-physician contractual arrangement, see Chapter 6.)

Interview with Medical Staff

In addition to discussing the financial considerations and other specifics of the practice with the administrator of the hospital, the physician will almost certainly want to speak to other physicians in the community. For this purpose, meetings with several supportive physicians, including the chief of staff, should be arranged. Here, it is very important to screen the medical staff members, so that nonsupportive physicians can be avoided. In their meetings with the physician, the medical staff members should emphasize the hospital's excellence and describe the support staff available, referral patterns, continuing education, conferences, and other medical matters that may be important issues for the physician.

Hospital Tour

The physician will obviously be interested in a tour of the hospital in which he will be working. This tour should be comprehensive but not exhaustive.

During it, the areas of greatest interest to the physician should be highlighted. For example, it would not be profitable to spend 30 minutes discussing the neonatal monitoring system with a psychiatrist candidate. Similarly, the alcohol detoxification center will be of little interest to a pediatric candidate.

The physician should meet as many key personnel as possible. One or two members of the medical staff should also join the administrator on the hospital tour. These individuals should be already briefed on the visit so that they can address the physician by name and be aware of his background. After the tour is completed, the physician should rejoin his wife (if she did not accompany him on the tour) and begin to explore the community.

Social Activities

The evening activities should be carefully planned so that the maximum number of interested and helpful medical and lay community individuals can meet with the physician and his spouse. If a cocktail party is appropriate, it should be scheduled together with a dinner afterward with selected individuals. If the physician is a sports enthusiast, someone with a similar interest should be included in the gathering. Again, it should be emphasized how important it is to accommodate the spouse and to make her feel welcome and included throughout the interview process. Women in the wife's age group, with similar interests and occupations, should be included in the activities to help her feel as comfortable and welcome as possible.

It is important to leave the impression with both the physician and his wife that there is much to do in the community and that there are available in the area many potential friends for both of them. The aim is to make them feel that relocating to the community would be a positive and comfortable move for all members of their family.

The schedule of activities should provide a comprehensive view of the community, without overwhelming or tiring out the physician and his wife. They should be allowed time to be alone so that they can discuss the input they have received and, if they choose to do so, tour the community on their own.

The success or failure of the interviewing process will largely depend on the people that are involved in the recruitment effort and how well they present the medical opportunity, the community, and the available lifestyles.

Commitment to the Candidate

If the interview and area visit are proceeding well, the recruitment committee can next decide whether or not to offer a formal commitment to the candidate. If the committee decides that the candidate would be a welcome addition to the community, it should make an offer before the physician leaves the community. The committee should explain that a follow-up letter will be sent, detailing the specifics discussed and decided upon. The physician should leave the community with the feeling that he and the hospital have made a commitment to each other.

SUMMARY

The interview and area visit should be an enlightening experience for both the recruitment committee and the physician. The most positive result would occur when both the community and the physician see mutual areas of interest and wish to associate with each other. Although no one can guarantee the success of an area visit, if all of the various steps that we have described have been followed during the developmental and implementation phase of the physician recruitment program, the chances of success will be much improved.

Chapter 12

Follow-Up Steps and Strategies

FOLLOW-UP TASKS

After the interview and area visit have been completed, the recruitment process must be completed by extensive follow-up activities to achieve a smooth transition and permanent retention of the recruited physician. This requires careful attention to details. After the departure of the physician, the recruitment commitment should be finalized in the following steps.

The first step should be a written letter to the physician documenting what was discussed verbally. The letter should explain how much everyone concerned enjoyed the physician's area visit and how much the community and hospital are looking forward to the physician's relocation. It should also note how eager the hospital is to be of assistance. A letter of agreement should be included. This letter should be sent to the physician immediately after the first visit.

Within a few days following the letter, the physician should be contacted by phone. In this call, the hospital's interest in the physician should be confirmed. In turn, the hospital should attempt to obtain a commitment from the physician with a timetable of his plans. At this point, the physician's questions and requests for further information should be answered as promptly as possible.

Once the physician has made a commitment his signed agreement should be obtained as soon as possible. An individual should be assigned to the physician and his family to serve as liaison in handling the countless details involved in the period prior to the physician's relocation. There are many areas of concern that will require attention before the physician and his family physically relocate. It may be necessary for the physician to make a second site visit to attend to these matters. The most common areas of concern are:

- *Living accommodations.* Unless the physician already lives in the area, it will probably be necessary to find living quarters before he begins practice. The liaison person can be helpful in assisting the physician in this search. Some communities provide living accommodations for the physician and his family until the practice becomes self-supporting.
- *Schools and religious affiliations.* The liaison person should discuss preferred school arrangements with the physician, then secure and mail the necessary applications. Also, information about churches or synagogues in the area should be sent to the physician. In this way, much of the detail work on these matters can be completed prior to the beginning of the new practice.
- *Spouse occupation and interest.* If the spouse is working, the liaison person can arrange for her to be aware of new employment opportunities. She can also be apprised of educational opportunities and local museums, clubs, and hobbies. Again, it should be emphasized how important the spouse and family are in the relocation process.
- *Community support.* The aid of the community should be enlisted in welcoming the physician and his family. This is especially important in medically underserved areas. If the community is too demanding or if patients do not pay their bills or unduly burden the physician, it may soon find itself again without a physician. The assistance in this regard can be enlisted from hospital and community public relations groups, from newspaper articles, in civic and religious meetings, or from whatever other sources the recruitment committee feels would be feasible to explore.
- *Banking.* An important question is where and how the physician will do his personal and business banking. The committee should have available a list of those banks with the most competitive interest rates, services, and conveniences. It should also be prepared to offer advice on what types of accounts the physician will need. The liaison person should arrange for endorsement stamps, deposit-by-mail envelopes, and other small but important banking aids the physician will need.
- *Medical staff support.* A hospital physician should be assigned as a liaison person between the recruited physician and the medical staff. A peer with whom the physician can discuss options and specifics can help the physician feel more at ease and comfortable at the hospital.
- *Establishing a practice.* The question of the office location and the method of acquiring it should be explored prior to the physician's relocation, but the specifics will now have to be discussed with the physician. The location's proximity to the hospital and other medical facilities and its convenience and accessibility for both physician and patients should be taken into account when selecting a practice site.

- *Practice structure.* It should be decided whether the practice will be with an existing physician (partnership), a professional corporation, or that of a private practitioner.
- *Start-up funds.* The amount of start-up money needed will be influenced largely by the agreement. The amount must be calculated for six to twelve months. It should cover rent, salaries, utilities, supplies, postage, printing, auto operation, taxes, insurance, cleaning, and maintenance. It should take into account repayments and all personal living expenses.
- *Office personnel.* The liaison person can serve as a coordinator for selecting and preinterviewing office staff. The selected individuals can then be presented to the physician for his approval.
- *Equipment and supplies.* The liaison person should compile a comprehensive list of all equipment and supplies required by the physician. This will save the physician much time and aggravation.
- *Insurance.* Insurance coverage requirements vary from state to state. It is wise therefore to check with a local attorney and accountant on this subject. However, the following types of insurance are standard: malpractice, disability, life, health, public liability, car, fire, theft, employee, and comprehensive.
- *Office systems.* Procedures should be set up to handle billing, credit and collections, appointments, filing, bookkeeping, accounts payable, and personnel records. The liaison person should present the appropriate office systems to the physician for his selection and approval.
- *Professional assistance.* The liaison person should recommend an attorney, an accountant, and a banker who can render professional services when necessary.
- *Legal necessities.* There are many licenses, certificates, and workmen's compensation forms that are required to begin a practice. These should be completed prior to the physician's relocation.
- *Hospital privileges.* Procedures for obtaining hospital privileges should be initiated six months in advance, since most hospitals have a fairly involved credentials process. If there is more than one hospital in the area, it may be appropriate to have the specialty physician obtain privileges at more than one facility.

THE TRANSITION PERIOD

After a carefully planned physician recruitment program, a physician has decided to relocate and begin a new practice. It is now tempting to relax and anticipate the increased census the new physician will generate. However, the responsibility of the physician recruitment committee does not end when a physician signs a contract with the hospital. The transition period—approximately the first three months of practice—should now become the central focus of the committee.

There are many aspects to consider in establishing a practice and relocating to a new community. During the follow-up phase, the administrative details of initiating a practice should have been completed. Now, by assisting in the preparation and organization of the practice, the prospects of a smooth transition for the physician and the hospital are greatly increased.

Assisting the New Physician

There are many ways to help a physician during the transition and beginning phases of his practice:

- If there is a long delay before the physician initiates his practice, arrangements should be made to have the local newspaper delivered to his home town. This will help the new physician and his family become acquainted with the community.
- If feasible, a picture of the new physician should be distributed to the hospital employees so that, when he begins practice, the staff will recognize his name and face.
- If the new physician is a surgeon, the operating room supervisors should be contacted to make sure their relationship with the physician is working smoothly. The physician himself should be contacted after his first case to verify that everything is satisfactory.
- Each department head should be personally encouraged to adopt a favorable attitude toward the physician.
- A meeting should be arranged with the physician after a few weeks to determine if there are any problems or complaints.
- Periodic dinners with the physician and his spouse can cement the relationship with the hospital.
- If the physician has a special medical interest, arrangements can be made for him to deliver a lecture at the hospital for the physicians in the area.

Generating New Patients

Unless the new physician assumes an established practice, he will be extremely concerned about his patient base. The physician will thus most likely require assistance in the several direct and indirect methods of generating new patients.

The indirect methods include exposure to the medical and general communities by attending conferences and conventions; accepting teaching positions; giving speeches and lectures at hospitals, religious centers and civic groups, and through speaker's bureaus; and actively utilizing the public relations of the hospital by participating in free screening clinics or health fairs the hospital sponsors.

The direct methods of generating new patients include placing the physician on the hospital's emergency room panel or back-up roster and encouraging the workmen's compensation board and industrial clinics and centers to send their patients to the physician.

It is important to assure the physician that there are patients who are seeking his services, thus minimizing the risk of failure and enhancing the probability of retention.

RETENTION OF THE PHYSICIAN

It is important to have an ongoing relationship between the administrator and the recruited physician. The physician should not be ignored after he begins practice, with the administrator and committee assuming that all is well. Situations might develop six months into the practice that can cause serious problems for the physician, that can affect his productivity and, in turn, the hospital's revenue. If the administrator keeps in touch with the physician, efforts can be made to solve such problems before they become serious. Indeed, the retention process continues throughout the physician's career with the hospital.

The retention function is especially important in rural facilities. Physician retention can be a particularly difficult task for a rural facility. In 1978, a study of 67 physicians was conducted to determine their reasons for establishing or leaving practices in rural areas. The results are shown in Table 12–1.

Three factors were found to be common among the various reasons given by the physicians in the study. (1) Good professional support is mandatory for successfully maintaining a small community practice. (2) A physician's predisposition to small community living is essential in the recruitment of that physician for rural practice. (3) There are substantial differences in the demographic characteristics of persons who desire to practice medicine in a rural area. Of the physicians in the study, 72 percent left the rural practice due to economic, social, and professional logistical reasons. In general, the apparent geographical mobility seemed to stem from an unsatisfactory professional situation.[1]

The main thrust of the retention strategy in a rural area should therefore be to improve the professional aspects of the medical practice, thereby enhancing the flow of physicians to the rural community. A recent report pre-

Table 12-1 Reasons for Leaving Medical Practice in a Rural Community

Percentage of respondents giving reason	Professional logistical reasons
60	I wished to change my type of practice.
57	The opportunities for professional growth were limited in that medical community.
50	I eventually developed the feeling that the private practice of medicine there was a dead-end job.
49	I was unable to rely on the physicians in that medical community for much professional support.
43	Emergency calls became quite a problem
43	The professional and educational opportunities I desired were not available in that community.
41	There was insufficient time off from my practice.
41	I was unable to participate adequately in postgraduate (continuing) medical education for myself.
22	Health care facilities for my patients, other than in my office, were lacking.
17	The resources of the hospital were too limited.
16	The distance from my office to the hospital was too great.

	Economic reasons
35	The amount of work I had to do to achieve reasonable income was excessive.
33	The geographical area in which I practiced yielded too limited an income.

	Social reasons
40	The resources of the community were limited.
39	The small-town mentality and gossiping irritated us.
39	There were too few peers to relate to socially and intellectually.

Source: Ralph C. Parker and Andrew A. Sorenson, "The Tide of Rural Physicians: The Ebb and Flow, or Why Physicians Move out of and into Small Communities," *Medical Care* 16, no. 2 (© February 1978): 155. Used by permission.

---

pared for the Department of Health, Education, and Welfare by the Rand Corporation suggests several methods for enhancing the professional situations of rural medical practitioners: (1) automated systems of professional support to connect the rural physician with the clinical resources of large medical centers and thereby reduce the sense of isolation; (2) income tax incentives to encourage physicians to practice in underserved areas; (3) and continuing education and professional development programs for rural physicians, sponsored by organizations such as the regional medical programs (as recently demonstrated in Missouri).[2]

A variation on the second recommendation is found in several recent state laws that afford medical school loan forgiveness on the basis of geographical location of practice.[3] Experience to date however indicates that such programs are only minimally effective. For example, although medical students were given $155 million in scholarships and low interest loans during the past decade through the Health Professions Student Assistance Program alone, only 86 physicians who received such support "had portions of their loans cancelled in return for establishing practices in designated shortage areas."[4]

The third recommendation of the Rand study—continuing education programs directed to physicians practicing in rural areas—has been implemented in many communities. A recent example is the sponsorship of such a program by the University of Kentucky Medical Center in collaboration with the local comprehensive health planning council.[5]

An administrator of a rural hospital should examine all these strategies when developing a program for physician retention. Addressing these issues before the actual recruitment takes place can improve the chances of recruitment and retention of physicians in rural communities. (The retention problem is discussed in greater detail in Chapter 14.)

A case study of the external recruitment process highlighting the interview, area visit, and resulting retention of a physician seeking a location is presented in Appendix A.

NOTES

1. Ralph C. Parker and Andrew A. Sorenson, "The Tide of Rural Physicians: The Ebb and Flow, or Why Physicians Move out of and into Small Communities," *Medical Care,* February 1978, p. 155.

2. Rand Corporation, *Administrative Report Prepared for the Department of Health, Education and Welfare,* AR–691–HEW, June 29, 1972, p. 73.

3. C.S. Presser, "Factors Affecting the Geographic Distribution of Physicians," *Journal of Legal Medicine* 3 (1975): 12.

4. *Internal Medical News,* September 1, 1974, p. 26.

5. F.D. Scutchfield et al., "Physician Recruitment: The Responsibility of the Community Medical School and Planning Council" (Paper presented at the American Medical Association conference on rural health, Detroit, April 1974).

Part III

Implementation of the Physician Recruitment Process—Internal Recruitment

Not all hospitals will experience the same physician recruitment needs. As indicated in the previous chapters, many hospitals must attract physicians from outside the area in order to increase their medical staff. In other cases, hospitals may wish to recruit physicians from within the existing medical community to augment their medical staffs. Such an "internal" approach may be the solution for a hospital located in an area that is oversupplied with physicians yet is not receiving an adequate amount of patient referrals. A common dilemma for hospitals today is how to deal with a physician over-supply and a declining patient census. What can a hospital do to resolve this situation and increase its market share?

Chapter 13

The Internal Recruitment Committee

As indicated in the first part of the book, the initial step in the recruitment process is to establish the planning committee to perform physician need and market analyses. After these have been completed, the committee must determine to what extent the hospital will be involved in the internal recruitment process. The final step in the planning process, determining the financial commitment, is most important. It is crucial to know how much money is available for the recruitment process. In an internal recruitment program, money will not be needed for area visits by physicians coming from geographical locations more than 30 miles away. Rather the financial commitment will involve such items as the hiring of executive search people, entertainment for physicians and their families, and basic public relations and promotion.

Still, it is difficult to know how much financial support will be necessary before embarking on an internal recruitment program. It is therefore advisable, after obtaining a commitment for the program, to establish a basic fund for financial requirements and then to monitor this fund on a weekly basis for a one-month period. By the end of the period, it should be possible to develop a budget for the additional funds needed for future recruitment efforts. The committee should be apprised of the financial situation and given a statement of how the recruitment money is being spent.

The next phase in internal recruitment is the same as in external recruitment: the formation of the recruitment committee. The same member roles must be defined, but this time the purpose is to recruit physicians from within the area, specifically from among those physicians who are presently on the hospital's active staff but are not referring significant numbers of patients to the facility.

The recruitment committee should consist of approximately five to seven members representing hospital administration, the governing board, the medical staff, and the community.

ADMINISTRATOR

The hospital administrator is the leader in the internal recruitment process. The administrator's role is to coordinate all efforts of the committee. The administrator should rely on and seek the assistance of other committee members, including the director of professional relations if available, but should assume the leadership role in carrying out the various tasks.

As we have seen, the administrator is responsible for the initial stages of the recruitment program, including the establishment of the planning committee. In most cases, the administrator also has the major role in need determination and marketing analysis. In addition, the administrator should be closely involved with the hospital's active staff (details of this function are presented in the following chapter). The administrator should develop the active medical staff profile, which shows physician activity, ages, and admissions. These data will provide the committee with information as to where problems exist in hospital activity and will assist in targeting strategies to increase physician referrals.

The administrator must serve as a support person for the medical staff, maintaining an attitude of openness and approachability. If the administrator merely sits behind closed doors, the fact that the hospital's physicians are dissatisfied might never be known. The physicians may not be admitting patients to the hospital because their parking lot is always filled with unauthorized automobiles or because a nurse has antagonized a physician in a minor incident. In such situations, the administrator should serve as a sounding board for the physician's problems, needs, and suggestions.

The administrator should be visible daily so that the staff can see that administration is taking an active interest in the hospital's operations. This also serves to notify administration if a problem arises and to enable it to handle it with dispatch.

The administrator should arrange to eat breakfast or lunch in the physicians' dining room. This provides an opportunity to socialize informally with the physicians. If the medical staff is large, the key physicians should be approached and questioned as to the efficiency of the hospital and any complaints regarding the facility. If the medical staff is small, the administrator can contact each physician personally, expressing interest in each individual's opinions and needs. The administration should emphasize that it is interested in knowing about the physicians' problems and would appreciate honest and constructive comments.

The administrator should regularly attend medical staff meetings, in order to be apprised of grievances or suggestions, and should meet with the heads of departments and the chiefs of staff on a regular basis. On such occasions, equipment and other needs can be frankly discussed.

The administrator should attend social and sporting events with the physicians. This can promote a feeling of camaraderie between the administration and the medical staff. Casual events are sometimes the best situations in which to share feelings and opinions. For example, the administrator could sponsor an annual event as a way of saying thank you to the physicians for their loyalty. At the professional level, arrangements could be made for key physicians to attend continuing medical educational seminars and conventions. Efforts could be made to initiate or improve the continuing medical education at the facility, for example, by working with other facilities in presenting stimulating speakers and seminars.

Upon learning of specific problems the physicians may have, the administrator should attempt to remedy them as soon as possible. If the problems are small and within the administration's scope of authority, they should be acted upon quickly, and the physicians should be told exactly what has been done. If the problem is a major one, the matter should be brought to the board of directors as soon as possible. If the request for solution is reasonable, the administrator should push for a speedy decision. Red tape and bureaucratic entanglements can cause disillusionment among the medical staff. The administrator should be receptive to new ideas and keep lines of communication open to the physicians.

Considering all these internal recruitment responsibilities and tasks, the burden on the administrator might seem to be overwhelming. It is important to remember, however, the underlying purpose of all these functions is to ensure a productive ongoing relationship with the staff physicians. The physicians should feel comfortable in coming to the administrator with problems at any time, knowing that immediate action will be taken to remedy the situation.

Only recently has marketing been incorporated as a normal part of hospital operations. Hospital administrators may, however, not be comfortable with their new marketing role, despite its importance. In such cases, there should be an assistant or a medical staff person who can perform a large share of the marketing tasks and responsibilities for the administrator.

MEDICAL STAFF MEMBERS

The medical staff plays an integral role in ensuring the effectiveness of an internal recruitment program. The medical staff members on the internal recruiting committee are responsible for convincing their peers and associates that the facility is worth supporting. It is very important that the medical staff members on the recruiting committee share this opinion with other medical staff members.

The medical staff member should speak with other physicians in the community to promote support for or affiliation with the hospital. It is important that this member act to counter any preconceived negative ideas other physicians may have about the hospital, administration, or other staff members.

The medical staff member should monitor the ongoing activities of the individual staff physicians, targeting potential problems and any decreases in activity at the initial stages. If a medical staff member is considering changing hospital affiliation, it becomes the responsibility of the medical staff committee member to discuss the reasons with the physician, possibly with the result that he changes his mind. The committee member should identify other supportive medical staff who can assist in these responsibilities. With such a network of supportive medical staff at the hospital, immediate feedback on the existence of problems and, thus, continuing positive internal recruitment can result.

COMMUNITY MEMBERS

In the external recruitment process, community involvement was an important factor in arranging physician visits to the community. In the internal recruitment process, community involvement takes the form of promotion. It is important that the physicians affiliated with the hospital recognize the hospital's position in the community and its growth potential.

In this context, the community leader on the recruitment committee should take the lead in promoting physician relations in the community. This member can assist in newsletter production and in the writing of stories that highlight the hospital's activities. If the hospital is planning a health fair or a fund-raising event, the community member may be able to provide assistance in the activity's development and implementation.

GOVERNING BOARD MEMBER

The governing board member on the recruitment committee serves as a prestigious resource and support person. Members of the governing board are normally not involved with the medical staff, except when a board member attends a regular monthly meeting. Therefore, when a governing board member is a member of the recruitment committee and takes an active role in talking with various medical staff members, he provides the physicians with a greater feeling of board commitment and support. Such board representation gives the physicians the feeling that there is a genuine commitment by the hospital to improve the facility.

Specifically, the governing board member of the committee should provide support to the hospital administrator and serve as a liaison between the governing board and the recruitment committee. Since the governing board has the responsibility of deciding where the dollars will be spent, the governing board member's presence on the committee indicates to the physicians that the hospital is listening to their requests and needs on an ongoing basis. In this way active staff support for the hospital will be easier to maintain and strengthen.

Chapter 14

Retention of the Active Staff

Assume that a hospital has a medical staff of 100 physicians; however, census is dropping each day, and grumblings and complaints are heard in the physicians' dining room. What can be done to remedy this all-too-familiar situation? A strong and communicative rapport with the medical staff could help to avoid such a situation. However, if the problem is at hand or if the administrator simply recognizes the need to strengthen relationships with the hospital's physicians, the hospital should move to remedy the problem by (1) developing an active medical staff profile and (2) conducting interviews with active staff members.

THE ACTIVE MEDICAL STAFF PROFILE

Active participation by medical staff members, through admissions and through referrals to other physicians, will determine to a large extent the future of the service area's health care system and the hospital's growth. Therefore, in order to develop an internal recruitment plan, it is necessary for the administration to know as much as possible about the hospital's physicians.

Using a marketing approach, an analysis of the hospital's activity statistics should be conducted. The analysis should determine the number of physicians on staff, how many are currently heavy admitters, how many used to be heavy admitters, and when the last admission was for each physician.

A sample active medical staff profile resulting from such an analysis is presented in Tables 14-1, 14-2, 14-3, and 14-4. The information for this profile was compiled from information provided by a hospital's medical staff secretary and from interviews and research by the hospital's medical records department. The profile is of the active staff only; it excludes radiologists, pathologists, and other nonoffice-based physicians.

Table 14–1 Percentage Comparison of Active Staff with All U.S. Physicians by Age Group

Age	Total Active Staff	Hospital Active Staff Percentage	Percentage of All U.S. Physicians[a]
Under 34	2	2.2%	26.8%
35–44	29	32.2	24.7
45–54	32	35.6	21.2
55–64	21	23.3	14.3
Over 65	6	6.7	13.0
Total	90	100.0%	100.0%

[a] From the American Medical Association, *Profile of Medical Practice,* © 1980, p. 140. Used by permission.

Source: Hyatt Medical Enterprises, *Management by Objectives Program,* 1977, p. 53.

Table 14–2 Longitudinal Record of Admissions by Specialty, Active Staff

Specialty	1976	1977	1978	1979
Medicine	2,162	2,480	2,944	3,071
Surgery	1,675	1,881	2,116	1,981
Orthopedics and orthopedic surgery	963	994	1,022	899
OB/GYN	1,570	1,605	1,558	1,426
FP/GP	1,623	1,428	1,331	1,390
Total	7,993	8,388	8,971	8,767

Source: Hyatt Medical Enterprises, *Management by Objectives Program,* 1977, p. 54.

As can be seen in these tables, there are three main areas that must be examined in order to complete an active medical staff profile: age, admissions by general/family practitioners, and admissions by specialty and sub-specialty.

Table 14-3 Active Staff by Subspecialty, Number of
Physicians, Average Age, and Total Admissions, 1979

Subspecialty	No. of M.D.'s	Average Age	No. of Admissions
Medicine			
General Medicine	10	50.5	1,407
Cardiology	4	41.0	548
Dermatology	1	36.0	1
Gastroenterology	2	44.0	491
Neurology	2	37.5	150
Nephrology	1	38.0	28
Pulmonary Disease	1	56.0	106
Psychiatry	4	50.0	283
Pediatrics	4	51.3	57
Surgery			
General Surgery	9	52.3	749
Cardiothoracic	3	45.0	48
Neurosurgery	2	44.0	53
Ophthalmology	3	42.0	116
Otorhinolaryngology	4	47.0	659
Plastic Surgery	1	68.0	68
Proctology	1	42.0	85
Urology	4	52.0	186
Vascular Surgery	3	57.0	20
Orthopedics and Orthopedic Surgery	10	50.6	899
OB/GYN	10	50.2	1,426
FP/GP	13	57.7	1,390
Total	92		8,770

Source: Hyatt Medical Enterprises, *Management by Objectives Program,* 1977, p. 55.

Age

An analysis of the age of the active medical staff, relative to the general
physician population, is an important factor to consider in planning an internal recruitment program. For example, if 60 percent of a hospital's medical
staff is 65 years or older, the facility has a potentially critical problem and
must begin immediately to look to the existing medical community for additional support. A format for showing the age distribution of the medical staff
is presented in Table 14-1.

Table 14-4 Average Number of Admissions Per Physician by Specialty, Active Staff, 1976–1979

	1976 Number of			1977 Number of			1978 Number of			1979 Number of		
	Adms.	M.D.'s	Avg.	Adms.	M.D.'s	Avg.	Adms.	M.D.'s	Avg.	Adms.	M.D.'s	Avg.
Medicine	2,162	24	90.1	2,480	29	85.5	2,944	29	101.5	3,071	29	105.9
Surgery	1,675	28	59.8	1,881	28	67.2	2,116	28	75.6	1,981	28	70.8
Orthopedic and orthopedic surgery	963	10	96.3	994	10	99.4	1,022	10	102.2	899	10	89.9
OB/GYN	1,570	9	194.4	1,605	10	160.5	1,558	10	155.8	1,426	10	142.6
FP/GP	1,623	13	124.8	1,428	13	109.8	1,331	13	102.4	1,390	13	106.9
Total average number of admissions per physician			95.2			93.2			94.7			97.4

Source: Hyatt Medical Enterprises, *Management by Objectives Program*, 1977, p. 56.

Admissions by General/Family Practitioners

It is important to know where the primary care admissions are going. Are referral patterns changing? Is there one specialist who is receiving the majority of primary care referrals? A review of such data can indicate which specialists are obtaining the majority of referrals and how these patterns are changing over time.

Admissions by Specialty and Subspecialty

It is also important to determine for internal recruitment purposes which specialists have admitted patients in the preceding three to five years. In this connection, referral patterns should be closely analyzed. Are patients admitted under primary care physicians' or under specialists' names? In another situation, a hospital may discover that its orthopedic surgical admissions have declined over a three-year period and may wish to offer expanded services in the subspecialties to correct the decline. Formats for the display of information on admissions by the specialty active staff, by subspecialty and average number of admissions per physician, are shown in Tables 14–2, 14–3, and 14–4.

INTERVIEWS WITH ACTIVE MEDICAL STAFF MEMBERS

Another integral part of the process of retaining active staff members is the medical staff interview. To develop a clearer understanding of how the hospital is viewed by physicians, interviews should be conducted with as many active staff members as possible, and also with physicians who are not

Exhibit 14-1 Physician Interview for Internal Medical Staff Analysis

Physician Name: _____ Interviewer: _____
Place of interview: _____
Date: _____

1. Are you satisfied with the care your patients receive at the _____ hospital?
   _____

2. Do any of your patients object to being hospitalized at _____ hospital?
   (If yes, find out why) _____

3. Are you satisfied with the overall performance of the ancillary services you use?
   _____

4. What can the hospital do, in your opinion, to improve its operation?
   _____

5. If you need something done by the hospital for you or your patient, who are you inclined to speak to?
   _____

6. Do you admit to other area hospitals? (If yes, why?)
   _____

7. What services do we currently lack that, if we had, would increase your utilization of _____ hospital?
   _____

8. If there were two things you could change about the _____ hospital, what would they be?
   _____

9. How far is your office from the hospital?

10. Are there other reasons that we have not discussed that you believe discourage you from using _____ hospital?
    _____

11. Do you decide where your patients will be hospitalized, or do you give your patients a choice?
    _____

12. Do you feel administration is responsive to medical staff requests?

13. Do you feel a part of the institution?
    _____

Source: Hyatt Medical Enterprises, *Management by Objectives Program,* 1977, pp. 61–62.

on the medical staff. The interviews should be indepth. They should solicit the personal perceptions and feelings of the primary admitters about the hospital and administration. A sample physician interview questionnaire is shown in Exhibit 14-1.

SUMMARY

Having developed an active medical staff profile and conducted interviews with each medical staff physician, the hospital will be armed with the facts required for efforts to retain its medical staff. The main thrust of active staff retention should be to generate active physician interest in the hospital and to bridge the potential communication gap between the staff physician and the administration. These efforts will enable the hospital to promote active staff retention and to increase overall utilization at the hospital.

Chapter 15

Nonactive Staff Utilization

The nonactive staff consists of those physicians who have either been on active staff and are no longer using the facility or who have never used the facility but are still potential admitters of patients to the hospital. In order to attract these physicians to the facility, it is important to adapt the efforts of the internal recruiting committee to tasks that will encourage nonactive staff utilization.

PROMOTIONAL MATERIAL

Promotional materials are probably the best means to attract physicians who are not presently on staff. It is easy to obtain a list of all physicians in the medical community. Of course, attempts to attract physicians away from nearby hospitals can put a strain on the relationship between the administrations of the facilities. One must be sensitive to this and produce materials that are professional, yet effective. A regularly distributed hospital newsletter can serve a very useful outreach function. The newsletter can feature the prominent physicians on staff in successive issues. It can describe ongoing events in the hospital and the community, explain growth patterns, and discuss relevant issues. In this way, the newsletter can become an excellent marketing tool.

In its initial stages, a monthly newsletter sent to physicians who are not connected with the hospital may end up in the trash can. The secret of its ultimate success as a promotional tool is the provision of repetitive, interesting stimuli. Such a newsletter will promote hospital recognition among nonactive staff physicians. This can serve as "a foot in the door" when approaching a physician about his potential utilization of the facility.

FOLLOW-UP CONTACTS

Following the distribution of the promotional material, a simple letter of introduction should be sent to the target physician. This letter need do little more than introduce the hospital and briefly discuss its services. It should refer to the newsletter or other promotional material, indicate that the physician is on the mailing list, and emphasize that, if he has any questions, he should contact the administrator immediately.

Two months later, a follow-up letter should be sent. This letter should convey more information on the hospital, including its plans and potential for growth. A month after that, if the physician has not responded, another letter should be sent, together with a self-response card. The letter should indicate that further information on the hospital is available to the physician, if requested. This information could deal with medical building concerns and medical staff planning projects and should be immediately available for sending to interested physicians.

Approximately six months after the initial written contact with the physician, the administrator should attempt to meet the physician personally to discuss the hospital's present status and plans for the future. If the hospital is contemplating building a medical building, that would provide the perfect entree for discussing potential tenancy. In sum, the more contacts nonactive physicians have with a hospital and administrator, the more likely productive relationships will evolve. High visibility and open communication are the best tools to promote such ongoing associations. In this respect, the internal recruitment of staff physicians should be a part of the hospital's day-to-day operations.

Part IV

Nonhospital Physician Recruitment

Recruitment for a private practice involves many of the same considerations encountered in recruitment for a hospital—the determination of need, a market analysis, a choice of the right program option, and a financial analysis. As in the case of a hospital recruitment program, the recruitment of a private practitioner may be done externally or internally with respect to the community. In all these respects, the functions of recruiting for a private practice are the same as those for a hospital—only on a different scale.

Chapter 16

Recruitment for a Private Practice

DEVELOPMENT PHASE

Determination of Need and a Market Analysis

Before a physician decides he needs an associate, he should review the steps involved in a determination of need (Chapter 2). How many physicians with the same specialty are practicing in the community? Are they active? Physician/population ratios will also impact on the potential success of an incoming physician. Though the majority of physicians have neither the resources nor the inclination to make a thorough needs determination, any knowledge regarding the existing medical community is beneficial.

Normally, it is not necessary for a private practitioner to perform a complete market analysis. It would, however, be useful for the physician to review the steps in preparing a market analysis (Chapter 3) to gain a better understanding of the medical community in which he practices.

Program Options

The option of employing a recruiting firm is worth considering in the case of a private practitioner who does not have the time required to conduct a full scale search program. The physician should review each of the four program options (Chapter 4) and then make his decision on the use of an outside firm. If he decides to employ one, he should examine the various types (Chapter 5), then select that type that best meets his recruitment needs.

Financial Considerations

The financial aspects of the recruitment process will be of primary concern to the private practitioner. This is a sensitive area that is difficult for the

195

physician to consider objectively. In most cases, the established practitioner has built a very successful and satisfying practice and is hesitant about offering large financial incentives to a new partner.

In this situation, the established practitioner should reevaluate his motives for bringing in an associate. If he is bringing in someone with whom he wishes to share the practice over the next several years, leading eventually to partnership on an equal basis, he should contact an attorney to draft an agreement that will phase the new physician into the practice and, within a specified period of time, provide the option of becoming a full partner. If the established physician does not intend to offer a partnership, he should determine a salary level that is competitive with other similar salaried positions and should, in very specific terms, delineate the responsibilities of the new physician.

Before recruiting a new associate, it is in the best interests of the established physician to talk not only with an attorney but also to a CPA to work out the financial aspects of the practice. This should be done before he interviews the first candidate. Many times a physician will feel overworked and, out of frustration and without preplanning, will place an ad in a specialty journal. If a qualified candidate responds and the physician has not prepared a recruitment package, the chances are that the candidate will not select that practice opportunity. The established physician may lose the very associate that he is trying to attract.

Preplanning in the financial area, ultimately translated into contractual terms, can promote an honest and productive long-term relationship between the established physician and the recruited candidate.

IMPLEMENTATION PHASE

External Recruitment Process

The private practitioner who is planning to recruit a physician into his practice must decide if he will recruit from within or from outside the local medical community. If he chooses to bring in a physician from the outside, he should rely on the market analysis of the community and then translate that information into a standard cover letter to prospective candidates. The letter should describe the existing community and the medical environment, explain the financial considerations, and contain a general statement as to why he is looking for a physician to associate with him. The physician should obtain brochures on the area from the local chamber of commerce and include these with the cover letter. The physician should then review the various physician sources (Chapter 8) and contact as many new physicians as possible.

The preinterviewing stage will be implemented primarily by telephone. If the physician decides to invite the candidate for an area visit, it will be necessary for him to consider travel expenses and other related interviewing costs. In any case, an interview will be necessary so that the physician can judge for himself the qualifications and personality of the interested candidate. If a mutual interest develops, the follow-up will be critical. A close review of the essential steps in the preinterview process (Chapter 10), the interview (Chapter 11), and the follow-up, transition, and retention phases (Chapter 12) will help the established physician to conclude successfully the external recruitment program.

Internal Recruitment Process

The internal recruitment process for a private practitioner will obviously differ in scope from that of a hospital. If the private practitioner decides to internally recruit a physician from the same area, the chances are good that he already knows practitioners in his specialty who reside in the community. Personal contacts with these physicians at meetings and lectures are good ways to inform them about the practice opportunity.

Contacting a physician that is already in practice locally entails entirely different circumstances than those involved in bringing in a physician from another area. The following should be considered when contacting the physician candidate:

- Status of the physician. Is the physician a salaried employee? Is he in private practice, an association, a partnership, or a multispecialty group?
- Size of the physician's practice. How many patients is the physician presently seeing? If he is in a salaried position or working for a health maintenance organization, will any of his patients be able to follow him into a new practice?
- Location of existing practice. Does the doctor presently practice a considerable distance away? If he must move, will the patients be able to follow him?
- Referral pattern. Who are the physicians who are presently referring to the physician? Would the physician lose his referral base if he were to move?

If these factors are considered before initiating the recruitment process, the established practitioner will not only save a great deal of time but also avoid many of the sensitive issues involved when contacting a physician already in practice.

Finally, it should be remembered that, whether the established physician decides to recruit a new physician from outside the community or from the existing community, he will need to perform the basic recruitment steps that include planning, assessment analysis, locating the interested physician, prescreening, interviewing, follow-up, commitment, and, finally, retention.

Chapter 17

Recruitment for Health Maintenance Organizations

A health maintenance organization (HMO) is a unique form of health care delivery. Four basic components differentiate the HMO from other modes of health care: An HMO is (1) an organized system providing (2) a comprehensive scope of health care services to (3) a voluntarily enrolled consumer population for (4) a prepaid fixed fee.[1]

HMOs, which emerged 40 years ago, have grown considerably in the past 10 years, from fewer than 40 to 238 plans.[2] This increase was spurred by the Health Maintenance Organization Act of 1973 (Public Law 93–222), which stated that "each employer which is required during any calendar quarter to pay its employees the minimum wage ... and which during such calender quarter employed an average number of employees of not less than 25, shall ... include in any health benefits plan offered to its employees ... the option of membership in qualified health maintenance organizations .... "[3]

HMO MODELS

There are three HMO models: staff, prepaid group practice, and individual practice association. Each model is characterized by the type of relationship between the physicians who deliver the service to the member and the legal corporate entity, the HMO.

Staff Model

In the staff model, the physicians are organized as employees who devote 100 percent of their practices to the HMO. All income (prepayments and any fee-for-service revenues) accrues to the HMO, and the employees are compensated through an arrangement other than fee-for-service, such as by a salary or retainer. The physicians generally practice together as a group in a centralized facility and share common support personnel, medical records, and equipment. The HMO must provide or arrange for continuing education. The staff model is also referred to as a "closed panel," because enrollees may select only from among the HMO physicians to receive contracted physician service benefits.[4]

Medical Group Model

In the medical group arrangement, the physicians and other licensed health professionals are organized as a partnership, professional corporation, or other association that executes an agreement or contract with one or more HMOs. Though the physicians are not salaried employees or "staff" of the HMO, this model is still considered a closed panel. As their principal professional activity (more than 50 percent individually), the physicians engage in a coordinated practice. As a group, they devote over 35 percent of their aggregate activity to the delivery of health services to the HMO members. Like the staff model, the medical group model shares records, equipment, and professional, technical and administrative staff and provides continuing education. The HMO compensates the medical group at a negotiated per capita rate for the enrollment it serves. This income is then distributed to the individual group members according to a prearranged schedule.[5]

Individual Practice Association Model

As the HMO concept began to attract large numbers of patients, individual physicians developed their own version of the HMO—the individual practice association (IPA). An IPA is a partnership, association, corporation, or other legal entity that delivers, or arranges for the delivery of, health services. The entity accepts a capitation rate and a degree of risk. It enters into written service arrangements with health professionals who provide their services in accordance with a compensation procedure established by the entity. This model differs from the other two in that the physicians continue to practice in solo or group settings, maintaining their private offices. Since many IPAs were originally sponsored by local medical societies as foundations for medical care, most of the physicians in the area were usually invited to participate. Thus, the IPA became associated with the concept of an open-panel practice. However, membership in an IPA does not limit a physician's practice to the treatment of HMO enrollees.

The compensation arrangement may be fee-for-service. To reconcile fee-for-service compensation for the physicians with the fixed prepaid revenue the HMO receives from enrollees, the physician agrees to a fee schedule and accepts a degree of financial risk. For example, the physician may agree to accept 85 to 90 percent of his regular fee, and the balance will be held in a reserve pool to provide a financial cushion. At year-end, if utilization has been within the projected parameters, the physicians might receive up to 100 percent of their claims, after reserve contingencies. If money runs low, the physician may agree to accept a pro rata decrease in fees and may be liable for inappropriate hospital costs. The association either pays hospital costs itself or teams up with an insurance carrier.

Because of their decentralized locations, IPA physicians share records, equipment, and staff only to the extent that is feasible. As in the other models, however, they must accept peer review of the appropriateness of their services.[6]

RECRUITING CONSIDERATIONS

Different recruiting considerations apply to the three HMO models.

Staff and Prepaid Group Practice Models

When recruiting a physician to an HMO, it is important to discuss the growth in HMOs over the past ten years and why so many people have turned to this option for their medical care. In view of skyrocketing hospital and medical costs, it is easy to understand the popularity of this type of delivery system. Today the 238 HMOs serve over 8.3 million Americans.

It is also important to acquaint the physician candidate with the concept and definition of an HMO. It should not be taken for granted that he understands or is familiar with the HMO concept. Brochures and articles should be available to explain particular aspects of the HMO and why it is a better choice for the physician than other options.

In the past, the idea of a physician practicing in an HMO had a negative connotation. An executive with Kaiser Foundation Health Plan, Inc., a leader in the prepaid field, has noted, however, that "most medical students today have a friendly bias towards HMO's."[7] It is in fact easier today to recruit physicians than it has been in the past.[8] For example, Kaiser's northern California region HMO recruits 150 new physicians each year, with an average turnover of only 10 percent during the first year of service.[9]

Physician Sources

The main source of new physicians for an HMO is the young physician who has just completed residency. This physician may have incurred training debts and may not be anxious to become involved in costly practice loans.

The various standard sources for other types of recruitment should be thoroughly investigated when recruiting for the HMO (see Chapter 8).

Advantages for Physicians

The HMO recruitment committee should be prepared to explain to a physician candidate the following advantages of an HMO over a private practice.

No Costly Practice Start-Ups. To establish a private practice, a newly trained physician must rent or lease an office, hire personnel, obtain malpractice insurance, and engage in a variety of other necessary chores. He also must attract sufficient numbers of patients to support the practice and generate enough income to begin repaying debts incurred during medical training. If the physician joins an HMO, however, these problems are quickly eliminated.[10] Office space, personnel, equipment, insurance, and patients are all provided to the physician in a neat package. An especially important advantage for younger physicians is the assurance of a guaranteed income in the HMO, without the requirement of a personal investment.

Physician Productivity Is Maximized. The national ratio of physicians to the population is 1:700. Among HMOs the average ratio is 1:1,000.[11] This increased productivity is attributed to a greater use of support personnel, such as nurse practitioners and health educators. This enables the physician to practice a high level of medicine while the patients receive routine nonmedical care from the support staff.[12] In addition, the physician is relieved of many of the administrative and management responsibilities involved in a private practice, allowing him to concentrate solely on the practice of medicine.

Increased Quality of Care. For many physicians, the major attraction of an HMO is its quality of care. A recent study completed at the Johns Hopkins University in Baltimore, Maryland, reviewed the last 20 years of research on the quality of HMO care. The study found that "the quality of health care provided by HMO's is equal to or better than that provided by other delivery systems."[13]

The use of centralized medical records and personnel ensures the coordination of the HMO members' overall health care. Because a visit to the physician will not result in a large medical bill that might be a financial burden, HMO members are more likely to visit the HMO for routine preventive care. This is a significant factor in that it allows the physician to recommend care whenever it is necessary. On the other hand, HMO physicians do not fear the loss of patients and therefore do not prescribe unnecessary medication or treatment.

The peer review system associated with the HMO also functions to improve the quality of care. In the peer review meetings, staff physicians scrutinize each other's cases, especially those of hospitalized patients. Michael R.

Sopek, medical director of Prime Health Plan in Kansas City, Missouri, notes that this "isn't done with ill intent or malice. The doctors actually get to enjoy it. The sessions keep them refreshed, encourage them to share experiences. After a while, the doctor practices more cost-consciously by nature."[14]

Fewer Practice Hours. The HMO physician generally works 50–60 hours per week, which is comparatively less than the number of practice hours of their private practice colleagues. This is because the HMO physician has regular, known working hours, limited on-call responsibility, and paid vacations with adequate coverage. The fact that the HMO physician has more time for family, leisure activities, and continuing education is a strong recruiting factor.

Good Income. A survey of group/staff model HMO physicians shows that as primary care specialists—in general medicine, pediatrics, family practice, and internal medicine—HMO physicians earn an amount comparable to their peers in fee-for-service. Though the HMO cannot compete with the higher brackets in the fee-for-service sector, it is important to remind the physician candidate that, on the average, HMO physicians are able to spend more time practicing medicine, have fewer administrative responsibilities, have more paid time to pursue educational activities, have better structured after-hours call responsibilities, and often have better fringe benefits than their fee-for-service peers.[15] Finally, the point should be made that, instead of waiting for income from patients and insurance to reimburse the physician, the HMO physician receives payment immediately.

The Use of Part-Time Physicians. If an HMO is finding it difficult to attract full-time physicians, the use of part-time physicians should be considered. Physicians with large practices in the community can be given an opportunity to participate. If acceptable to the HMO, these physicians should be approached to continue care for the subscriber under the auspices of the HMO. Outpatient care can be rendered by such physicians either in the hospital's physical facilities or in the physicians' offices.

The physician does not have to make a full-time commitment to the HMO initially. If the capitation method of reimbursement is used, the HMO is required to reimburse the physician only on the basis of the actual number of subscribers enrolled. This differs somewhat from reimbursement on a salary basis, in which a set salary is earned by the physician, independent of the number of enrolled population. Under the salary method, the initial enrollment must be calculated, and an appropriate number of physicians must be employed. On the other hand, if enrollment figures do not meet enrollment expectations and if expensive full-time personnel are not fully utilized, the HMO might soon find itself in financial difficulty.

If the part-time physician supports the HMO concept, he can serve in a promotional role with regard to his fee-for-service patients. There is no need for him to make an initially broad commitment to the HMO; he need take only a few patients. At a later date, if he decides he does not want to participate further in the HMO method of health care delivery, he may relinquish his HMO patients. However, if the HMO concept is considered successful by the physician, he could, on a gradual basis and at his own election, become full-time.[16] This approach could help alleviate a physician shortage until full-time physicians are recruited.

Individual Practice Association Model

Recruiting for an IPA is somewhat different from recruiting for a staff or prepaid group model. The community's own physicians are the primary source for an IPA. New physicians in town who might appreciate the extra business and busy physicians who would be useful in marketing the program should be contacted as potential recruits. Other physician sources should, of course, also be explored (see Chapter 8).

The basic advantage for the physician in an IPA is private practice autonomy. The physician is able to continue his private practice as before without any disruption in service. The IPA patients are seen at times designated by the physician and usually do not account for more than 10 percent of his private practice. Unless a contract to the contrary has been signed, the physician is also free to drop out of the program without incurring a great financial loss.

The payment for care rendered to IPA patients is usually prompt and guaranteed. This can be an added bonus for a young physician in need of additional income.

The IPA can serve as an excellent source of patients necessary to build and maintain a practice. This is a useful recruiting tool to utilize in areas that are overcrowded with physicians.

Another advantage is that there is a large network of consultants available through an IPA. This provides opportunities for the IPA physician to meet new colleagues and contacts. In this context, there is also less worry for the physician that a referral to a consultant will be a financial burden for the patient.

Finally, the potential recruit should be reminded that, in the IPA, there is strength in numbers, that is, the purchase of supplies, insurance, equipment, and other resources can usually be obtained at good discounts. In short, the IPA physician enjoys the autonomy of private practice with the additional benefits of an HMO.

NOTES

1. Hospital Council of Southern California, *HMO Handbook,* January 1980, p. 1.

2. *Wall Street Journal,* April 3, 1981, p. 46.

3. *Public Law 93–222* (Health Maintenance Organization Act of 1973), December 29, 1973, Sec. 1310 (a).

4. Hospital Council, *HMO Handbook,* p. 2.

5. Ibid.

6. Ibid., pp. 2–3.

7. Margaret Leroux, "Pump $300 Million into Kaiser Growth," *Modern Health Care,* April 1980, p. 54.

8. Ibid.

9. Ibid.

10. Group Health Association of America, Inc., "Physicians, HMO's and Prepaid Medical Group Practice," (Washington, D.C.: Medical Directors Division, 1979), p. 1.

11. Hospital Council, *HMO Handbook,* p. 9.

12. Ibid.

13. Group Health Association, *Physicians, HMO's,* p. 2.

14. *Wall Street Journal,* p. 46.

15. Group Health Association, *Physicians, HMO's,* p. 5.

16. Samuel T. Wallace, "HMO's Don't Just Happen," *Journal of American Hospital Association,* June 1, 1974, p. 90.

Epilogue

There has been a great deal of conflicting information recently regarding physician recruitment efforts. It must be very confusing for an administrator of a health care institution to hear on the one hand that we are facing a potential physician surplus in the year 1990, yet on the other hand to be faced presently with a declining census and no immediate hope of alleviating the problem. The key to the dilemma is in the continuing problem of maldistribution. In fact, indications of severe physician shortages have, when the numbers were actually calculated, turned out to be problems of maldistribution rather than of shortages. And there is no guarantee that a coming surplus of physicians will alleviate the maldistribution problem. Hospitals that are presently suffering physician shortage problems or that see potential shortage problems in the future will not necessarily solve their problems by statistics that predict a physician surplus.

Still, it is crucial for administrators to plan for their hospitals' future growth and to include in these plans the need for additional physicians. If there is going to be a physician surplus, then the wise administrator should take advantage of that pending surplus by recruiting physicians who are compatible with the long-range plans of the institution. If there is no physician surplus, then it becomes even more important for the hospital to develop a physician recruitment program to ensure adequate medical staff coverage.

Case Study of an External Physician Recruitment

The importance of a comprehensive external recruitment program is illustrated in the following case study.

Doctor A. Jones, 29 years of age, has just completed a fellowship in gastroenterology at a well-known teaching hospital. He placed tenth in his graduating class at a major midwestern medical school. He is board-certified in internal medicine and board-eligible in gastroenterology. During his education and training, he incurred approximately $10,000 in long-term debts. Six months prior to completing his fellowship, he decided to investigate the potential of various areas in which he might establish his medical practice.

Doctor Jones is married and has a two-year-old child. His wife is an x-ray technician at the office of a local doctor. An outdoor enthusiast, Doctor Jones enjoys hiking, water sports, and skiing.

One of the first hospitals Doctor Jones investigated was City Memorial Hospital, located in a California beach community that provides a wide range of cultural, educational, and recreational opportunities. This 15-year-old hospital serves a community of 750,000 people and has a medical staff of 375 physicians, of which 150 are active, representing every major medical specialty. The hospital equipment is modern and comprehensive, and the hospital has just completed an expansion program.

Doctor and Mrs. Jones arrived at the community's metropolitan airport, obtained their luggage, and rented a car. The directions they had received on how to get to the hospital were difficult to understand, and Doctor Jones arrived late for his appointment with the hospital administrator. By that time, the administrator was in conference, creating another delay. The result was that the interview was hurried, and Doctor Jones was able to see only a

Source: Suzanne McNeely Lewitt, "Increasing Physician Referrals of Patients," *Health Care Review,* © May/June 1978. Used by permission.

portion of the hospital's facilities. During this time, his wife waited for him in the hospital waiting room.

To obtain information on housing, Doctor and Mrs. Jones stopped at the first real estate office they encountered. They were shown only expensive housing, and their impression was that living costs in the area were extremely high. In a visit to a friend of his medical school professor, a physician who had settled in the community, Doctor Jones inquired about City Memorial Hospital's medical environment. The physician, who had recently experienced some difficulties, was not enthusiastic about a new doctor's opportunities at the hospital. Doctor and Mrs. Jones returned home to evaluate the information they had received and assess their opportunities.

A second referral brought Doctor Jones to the Desert City Hospital. This 85-bed hospital, located in a rural area in the Mojave Desert, serves 30,000 people in the immediate area and about 10,000 more in surrounding farming communities. It has a staff of 20 physicians; the three oldest of these physicians are planning to retire within a few years. The hospital's equipment is adequate but not impressive. The hospital has had financial problems; it has a low occupancy rate of approximately 60 percent.

Upon their arrival at the airport, Doctor and Mrs. Jones were met by a member of the hospital board and driven to the best hotel in town. There, Mrs. Jones was greeted by the wife of another young physician on the hospital's medical staff, and the two proceeded to tour the shops and the recreational, and housing facilities in the area. During a luncheon at the home of a board member, Mrs. Jones met several other wives of the medical staff, board members, and hospital administration.

During this time, Doctor Jones was in conference with the hospital's administrator and two local physicians. In this meeting, he learned of the hospital's need for a general internist, the opportunities available in his subspecialty, and the economic advantages of practicing at the hospital. The administrator outlined the hospital's future economic plans and made an enthusiastic plea to Doctor Jones to "get in on the ground floor" of what promised to be a thriving and stimulating medical environment.

Afterwards, the administrator and Doctor Jones visited a potential office site. The doctor was also informed that one of the retiring physicians was willing to share office space with him, which would provide a basis for patient referrals.

That evening, Doctor and Mrs. Jones dined at the home of another physician and his wife and discussed the area's recreational facilities, its attractive child-rearing environment, its school system and cultural attractions, and the facilities available in nearby communities.

The next morning, the hospital administrator described to Doctor Jones the advantages of a position on the medical staff of Desert City Hospital and also indicated that there was an attractive employment opportunity for Mrs. Jones in the hospital's x-ray department. Following this meeting, Doctor Jones and his wife returned to their home to compare their practice opportunities.

Doctor Jones is now on the staff of Desert City Hospital. In spite of the fact that City Memorial Hospital had numerous advantages including the prestige and glamour of a big city hospital, Doctor Jones and his wife were impressed with the life style and the warm hospitality of the Desert City Hospital. The advantages offered by City Memorial were overcome by Desert City's carefully planned and executed physician recruitment program.

Doctor Jones' case is not unusual. Young physicians today are more critical of their alternatives than ever before. No hospital can rely on its reputation and location alone to attract new physicians. A carefully developed physician recruitment program is what makes the difference.

Index

A

Ability to pay for services rendered, 17
Accommodations, 170
Active medical staff, 25, 185-188
Activities
  physician, 5
  social, 166
Administrative responsibilities of
  physicians, 78-79
Administrator, 4, 33, 34, 37
  interview with, 163
  involvement of, 39
  level of expertise of, 34-35
  perspective of, 40-42
  on recruitment committee, 106-107,
    180-181
  review of hospital by, 38
Admissions
  by general/family practitioners, 188
  increasing of, 5
  office of, 24-25
  physician's last, 14
  by specialty and subspecialty, 188
  yearly, 14
Advertising, 112
  cost of, 39
Age
  of medical staff, 25, 188
  number of physicians by, 15
  of patients, 12

of physicians, 14
of population, 16
Agreements. *See* Contracts
Alien physicians, 8
Allocation of resources, 39
Allopathic medical schools, 8
AMA. *See* American Medical
  Association
Ambulatory care, 9
American Hospital Association, 76-101
American Medical Association
  (AMA), 9
  Center for Health Services Research
    and Development, 135
Analysis
  community, 13, 15-17
  community physician, 13, 15
  hospital, 12, 14-15
  market, 4, 21-32, 152, 179, 195
  medical staff, 40
  needs, 7
  patient age, 12
  physician need, 7
  qualitative, 7, 17-19
  quantitative, 7, 8-17
  of recruitment firms, 49-53
  of recruitment program, 4
Anesthesiology, 11
Assessment. *See* Analysis
Associations, 123-125
Attitudes of physicians, 26, 27

213

Availability
    of funds, 35-36
    of manpower, 7, 12, 22
    of medical services in area, 15
    of nurses, 22-23

B

Banking, 42, 170
BHP. *See* Bureau of Health
    Professions
Billings, 61
Board of directors
    See also Governing board members
    involvement of, 39
    joint conference committee of, 38
Bribes, 70, 72
Brochures, 64
Buddy system, 42
Budget for recruitment, 63-67
Bureau of Health Professions (BHP), 8
Business transactions, 70, 72
Byproduct firms, 49

C

Census trend seasonal variations, 26
Center for Health Services Research
    and Development, AMA, 135
Certified Public Accountants, 42
Child psychiatry, 11
Collections, 61
Commencement date and conditions,
    69
Commitment
    to candidate, 166-167
    financial, 179
    of interest, 153
Committees
    external recruitment, 105-110
    internal recruitment, 179-183
    joint conference, 38, 39
    planning. *See* Planning committee
    recruiting. *See* Recruitment

committee
Community
    See also Population
    ability of to pay for services
        rendered, 17
    analysis of, 13, 15-17
    information on, 18
    medical, 51
    needs of, 38
    relations with, 25
    support of, 170
    tour of, 162
Community members of recruitment
    committee, 109, 182
Community physicians, 114
    analysis of, 13, 15
Compensation methods, 91-96
Competition
    between hospitals, 25
    between physicians, 42
Conferences, 113
Congressional Office of Technology
    Assessment, 8
Consultant firms, 34, 48-49
Contacts
    follow-up, 4, 169-175, 192
    initial, 151, 162
Contracts, 79-81
    enforcement of, 69-70
    hospital-based physician, 74-75
    nonhospital-based physician, 67-74
    sample, 82-91
Cost per unit of service as method of
    compensation, 93-94
Costs, 35, 36, 45, 52
    advertising, 39
    brochure, 64
    entertainment, 39, 64-65
    equipment, 67
    guaranteed income, 66
    indirect, 60
    insurance, 66-67
    office help, 65-66
    office rental, 65
    patient care, 79
    printing, 64

recruiting firm, 39
relocation, 39
supply, 67
travel, 39, 64-65
Credentials checks on physicians,
  157-160
Criteria for selection, 33-37

D

Data
  community, 18
  hospital, 18
  population, 22
Date of commencement, 69
Declining market, 25-26
Delivery patterns, 18-19
Demand, 8
  determinants of, 146, 147-148
  fluctuation in, 26
  ratio of visits to, 11-12
Demographics, 16, 21
Departmental income percentage as
  method of compensation, 92-93
Determination
  of financial commitment, 179
  of need, 4, 7-19, 195
Development, 4, 195-196
Discounts
  office space, 23
  physician's, 73
Distribution of physicians, 9
Dues, 67

E

Economics
  in location preference, 146, 147
  neighborhood, 22
Educational background of population,
  16
Educational Commission for Foreign
  Medical Graduates, 137
Educational permits, 136

Emergency medicine, 11
Enforcement of agreements, 69-70
Engaged market, 25
Enrollment of medical schools, 8
Entertainment costs, 39, 64-65
Environment, 21-24, 146-147
  as factor in location preference, 145,
    146-147
  medical, 145, 147
Equipment, 171
  costs of, 67
Establishment of practice, 170
Ethnic background of population, 16
Evaluation. *See* Analysis
Examinations
  state, 131-134
  visa qualifying, 136-137
Executive search firms. *See* Placement
  agencies
Expenses for moving, 66
Expertise level of administrator, 34-35
External recruitment, 5, 196-197,
  209-211
  committee on, 105-110

F

Facilities use, 72-73
Family practitioner admissions, 188
Feedback, 4
Fees
  finder's, 49
  recruiting, 65
  search, 52
Financial assistance, 58-67
Financial commitment determination,
  179
Financial considerations, 57-101,
  195-196
Financial incentives, 59-62, 69
Financing methods, 41
Finder's fees, 49
First impressions, 162
Fluctuation in supply and demand, 26
FMG. *See* Foreign medical graduates

Follow-up, 4, 169-175, 192
Foreign medical graduates (FMG), 8,
   9, 26, 114-115, 136
Free office space, 23
Funds
   available, 35-36
   start-up, 171

G

General practitioner admissions, 188
Generation of new patients, 172-173
Geographic distribution of physicians,
   9
Geographic listing of medical schools,
   116-120
Glenn R. Frye Memorial Hospital, 58
GMENAC. *See* Graduate Medical
   Education National Advisory
   Committee
Goals. *See* Objectives
Governing board members
   See also Board of directors
   of planning committee, 4
   of recruitment committee, 107-108,
   182-183
Graduate Medical Education National
   Advisory Committee (GMENAC),
   8, 9
Graduates of foreign medical schools.
   See Foreign medical graduates
   (FMG)
Gross departmental charges percentage
   as method of compensation, 93
Group practices, 41
Guarantees
   income, 23, 41, 61-62, 66, 68, 94
   loan, 41, 62

H

Health and Human Services (HHS),
   23, 70
Health maintenance organizations

(HMO), 199-205
Health Maintenance Organization Act
   of 1973 (PL 93-222), 199
Health Professions Assistance Act of
   1976 (PL 94-484), 136
Health Professions Student Assistance
   Program, 175
Health systems agencies (HSA), 36, 50
Hematology, 11
HHS. *See* Health and Human Services
HMO. *See* Health maintenance
   organizations
Hospital
   affiliation with, 15
   analysis of, 12, 14-15
   competition between, 25
   data on, 18
   physician legal arrangements with,
   70-74
   physician's last admission to, 14
   primary affiliation with, 15
   proximity of one to another, 23
   recruitment firm relationship with,
   53-55
   rural, 175
   tour of, 165
Hospital-based physician agreements,
   74-75
Hospital privileges, 171
Hours, 24
HSA. *See* Health systems agencies

I

Immigration and Nationality Act, 136
Implementation, 4, 196-198
Incentives, 59-62, 69
Income
   guaranteed, 23, 41, 61-62, 66, 68, 94
   net departmental, 92-93
Indirect costs, 60
Individual practice association (IPA),
   200, 201, 204
Inert market, 24-25
Information. *See* Data

Initial contacts, 151, 162
Insurance, 43, 171
    costs of, 66-67
    malpractice, 41, 66
Interest commitment, 153
Interior decorator, 43
Internal recruitment, 5, 197-198
    committee on, 179-183
Interviews
    with active medical staff members, 188
    with administrator, 163
    with candidates, 41, 161-167
    with medical staff, 165
Investment of time, 35
IPA. *See* Individual practice association
Itinerary, 161-162

J

Joint conference committee, 38, 39
Journals, 112, 121-122

K

Kickbacks, 24, 70, 72

L

Last admission to hospital, 14
Laws. *See* Legislation
Lease, 95-96
Legal arrangements, 70-74
Legal necessities, 171
Legislation, 23, 50
    interpretations of, 70-72
Legitimate business transactions, 72
Licensure
    boards for, 113
    laws on, 50
    requirements for, 135-143
    restricted, 136

state, 131-134
Living accommodations, 170
Loans, 41, 62
Location
    office, 14, 15
    preferences for, 145-150
Long-range planning goals, 9
Ludlam, James E., 96

M

Malpractice insurance, 41, 66
Malpractice regulations, 50
Manpower
    availability of, 7, 12, 22
    studies on, 12-17
Market
    analysis of, 4, 21-32, 152, 179, 195
    declining, 25-26
    engaged, 25
    fluctuating, 26
    inert, 24-25
    negative, 24
    share of, 14
    undesired, 26
    unrealized, 25
Marketing, 3-4
    problems in, 24-26
Medical community, 51
Medical environment, 145, 147
Medical group model of HMO, 200
Medical meetings, 113
Medical schools, 111-112
    allopathic, 8
    enrollment of, 8
    foreign, 8, 9, 136. *See also* Foreign medical graduates
    geographic listing of, 116-120
    minority students in, 9
    osteopathic, 8
Medical societies and associations, 123-125
Medical specialty physicians, 10, 11
Medical staff
    See also Physicians

active, 185-188
age of, 25
analysis of, 40
concerns of, 18
interviews with, 165
involvement of, 39
nonactive, 191-192
on planning committee, 4
on recruitment committee, 108-109,
    181-182
relationship between recruitment
    firm and, 53
support of, 36, 170
survey of, 38
Medicare and Medicaid Antifraud and
    Abuse Amendments (PL 95-142),
    23, 70, 71
Methodology of planning, 4
Minimum income guarantee, 23, 41,
    61-62, 66, 68, 94
Minority students in medical schools,
    9
Mobility of population, 16
Models of HMOs, 199-204
Monthly newsletters, 191
Motivation of physicians, 26, 27
Moving expenses, 66
Musick, Peeler & Garrett, 96

N

National Board of Medical Examiners,
    137
National Center of Health Statistics,
    57
Needs
    analysis of, 7
    community, 38
    determination of, 4, 7-19, 195
    for medical services, 16
    of physicians, 26-27
    for physicians, 4, 7-19, 38, 41
    population, 7, 16
    for recruitment, 41
    short-term, 41

socioeconomic influences on, 22
Negative market, 24
Neighborhood economics, 22
    See also Community
Net departmental income percentage
    as method of compensation, 92-93
New patient generation, 172-173
Newsletters, 191
Nonactive medical staff utilization,
    191-192
Nonhospital-based physician contracts,
    67-74
Nonphysician health care providers, 8,
    9
Nurse-midwives, 8
Nurse practitioners, 8
Nurses
    availability of, 22-23
    recruitment of, 22
    shortage of, 22

O

Objectives
    long-range planning, 9
    of recruiting program, 38
    specification of, 4
    statistical, 7
Occupation of spouse, 170
Office help, 41, 60, 69, 171
    costs of, 65-66
Office location, 14, 15
Office of Program Integrity, 70, 72, 74
Office space, 41, 59, 69, 164
    cost of, 65
    discounted, 23
    free, 23
Office systems, 171
Office of Technology Assessment of
    Congress, 8
Oncology, 11
Opportunities, 26-27
Osteen, Arthur, 135
Osteopathic medical schools, 8
Osteopathic physicians, 113-114

Outline of recruitment program, 37
Outside firms, 34, 44
Overfunding, 62
Oversupply. *See* Surplus of physicians

P

Parking spaces, 24
Partnerships, 41
Patients
  admission of. *See* Admissions
  age analysis of, 12
  referrals of, 24
Patterns
  of health care delivery, 18-19
  of referrals, 15, 164
Permits, 136
Physician assistants, 8
Physician Distribution and Medical Licensure, 9, 11
Physicians
  See also Medical staff
  active, 25
  activity of, 5
  administrative responsibilities of, 78-79
  age of, 14, 15
  attitudes of, 26, 27
  community. *See* Community physicians
  competition between, 42
  contracts with. *See* Contracts
  credentials checks on, 157-160
  demand for, 8
  discounts for, 73
  geographical distribution of, 9
  hospital affiliation of, 15
  hospital-based, 74-75
  increasing of activity of, 5
  last admission to hospital by, 14
  medical specialty, 10, 11
  motivation of, 26, 27
  need for, 4, 38
  nonhospital-based, 67-74
  osteopathic, 113-114

population ratios to, 9-11
primary care, 10, 11-12
primary hospital affiliation of, 15
productivity of, 11, 12
profile of active, 25
reference checks on, 157-160
religious affiliations of, 170
retention of. *See* Retention of physicians
revenues generated by, 14
salaries of, 92
shortage of, 33
sources of, 38, 111-143, 201
specialties of, 10, 11, 14, 15
supply of, 8
surplus of, 8-9
PL 92-603 (Social Security Amendments of 1972), 71
PL 93-222 (Health Maintenance Organization Act of 1973), 199
PL 94-484 (Health Professions Assistance Act of 1976), 136
PL 95-142 (Medicare and Medicaid Antifraud and Abuse Amendments), 23, 70, 71
Placement agencies, 47-48
Planning
  long-range goals of, 9
  methodology of, 4
  reimbursement, 9
  stages of, 44
  strategic, 4
Planning committee, 4-5, 33, 57, 105, 179
  functions of, 7
Politics, 23-24
Poor reputation, 24
Population
  See also Community
  data on, 22
  demographics of, 16
  medical services needed or desired by, 16
  mobility of, 16
  needs of, 7
  physician ratios to, 9-11
  by physician and specialty, 15

Potential candidate sources, 38
Practice
   establishment of, 170
   group, 41
   opportunity for, 163
   private, 195-198
   structure of, 171
Preferences for location, 145-150
Preinterviewing stage, 151-160, 197
Prepaid group practice model of
   HMO, 201-204
Prescreening, 153-156
Preventive medicine, 11
Primary care physicians, 10, 11-12
Primary care visit/demand ratios,
   11-12
Primary hospital affiliation, 15
Printing costs, 64
Prior exposure as factor in location
   preference, 145, 146
Private practice, 195-198
Product, 3, 4
Productivity of physicians, 11, 12
Professional agencies, 41
Professional assistance, 171
Professional dues, 67
Professional journals, 112, 121-122
Professional organizations, 126-130
Professional staff support, 4
Profile of active medical staff, 25,
   185-188
Promotion, 3, 4, 191
Proximity to other hospitals, 23
Psychiatry, 11
Purpose. See Objectives

Q

Qualitative analysis, 7, 17-19
Quality of patient care, 79
Quantitative analysis, 7, 8-17

R

Rand Corporation, 174, 175
Ratios

physician/population, 9-11
   primary care visit/demand, 11-12
   yearly patient admissions/physician,
      14
Realtors, 42
Rebates, 70, 72
Receptionist, 24
Recruited physician characteristics, 16
Recruitment committee, 4, 39, 65
   administrator role on, 106-107,
      180-181
   community members of, 109, 182
   external, 105-110
   governing board member of,
      107-108, 182-183
   internal, 179-183
   medical staff members of, 108-109,
      181-182
   responsibilities of, 105-106
   role of, 33
Recruitment firms, 34, 44, 47-55, 195
   assessment of, 49-53
   costs of, 39
   fees to, 65
   hospital relationship with, 53-55
   medical staff relationship with, 53
   types of, 47-49
Recruitment of nurses, 22
Reference checks on physicians,
   157-160
Referrals, 24
   patterns in, 15, 164
Regionalization, 36
Regulatory agencies, 36, 50
Reimbursement plans, 9
Relationships
   recruitment firm-hospital, 53-55
   recruitment firm-medical staff, 53
   staff, 24
Religious affiliations
   of physician, 170
   of population, 16
Relocation costs, 39, 60
Reputation, 24
Residency programs, 111-112
Resource allocation, 39

Responsibilities
  administrative, 78-79
  recruitment committee, 105-106
Restricted licenses, 136
Retention of physicians, 4, 5, 173-175,
  185-188
  rate of, 36
Revenues generated per physician, 14
Review of hospital by administration,
  38
Roles
  of administrator, 106-107, 180-181
  of recruitment committee, 33
Rural hospitals, 175
Rural medical practitioners, 174

S

Salaries for physicians, 92
Sample contractual agreement, 82-91
Schools
  for children of physicians, 170
  foreign medical. *See* Foreign medical
    graduates
  medical. *See* Medical schools
Search consultant firms, 48-49
Search fees, 52
Seasonal variations in census trends,
  26
Selection criteria, 33-37
Service area, 21
Service cost per unit as method of
  compensation, 93-94
Share of market, 14
Shortage
  of nurses, 22
  of physicians, 33
Short-term recruitment needs, 41
Small geographic area health services
  9
Social activities, 166
Social Security, 71
Social Security Amendments of 1972
  (PL 92-603), 71
Societies, 123-125

Socioeconomic influences on health
  care needs, 22
Sources of physicians, 38, 111-143, 201
Specialties, 10, 11, 14, 15
  admissions by, 188
  number of physicians by, 15
  population by physician and, 15
  surgical, 10, 11
Specification of objectives, 4
Spouse of physician, 28, 41, 166
  occupation and interest of, 170
Staff model of HMO, 199-200, 201-204
Staff relationship, 24
Start-up funds, 171
State laws, 50
State licensure, 131-134
State medical societies and
  associations, 123-125
Statistical objective/needs analysis, 7
Strategic plans, 4
Structure of practice, 171
Subsidies, 62
Subspecialties, admissions by, 188
Supplies, 171
  cost of, 67
Supply and demand
  fluctuation in, 26
  for physicians, 8
Support
  community, 170
  medical staff, 36, 170
  office, 41
  professional staff, 4
Surgical specialty physicians, 10, 11
Surplus of physicians, 8-9
Survey of medical staff, 38

T

Technology, 24
Telephone calls, 151-153
Time investment, 35
Tours
  community, 162
  hospital, 165

Transition period, 171-173
Travel costs, 39, 64-65
Trends in census, 26

U

Undesired market, 26
United Business Publications, 113
University of Kentucky Medical
    Center, 175
Unrealized market, 25
Unsafe areas, 24
Utilization
    of health services, 23
    of hospital facilities, 72-73
    of nonactive medical staff, 191-192

V

Visa qualifying examination (VQE),
    136-137
Visit/demand ratios, 11-12
VQE. *See* Visa qualifying examination

W

Wunderman, Lorna, 135

Y

Yearly patient admissions/physician
    ratio, 14

About the Author

SUZANNE MCNEELY LEWITT is president of Medical Career Services, Inc., a physician recruitment company she founded in 1974 and which, two years later, became a part of Hyatt Medical Enterprises, Inc., a subsidiary of American Medical International, Inc. She received her bachelor of arts degree, *cum laude,* from California State University at Northridge, majoring in Communications.

Suzanne Lewitt has worked for over eight years in hospital marketing, including consultation with hospital boards and residency programs. She presents physician recruitment seminars nationally on a regular basis to health care professionals. She has also been a faculty member of the American Hospital Association.